Around the year

Brigitte Schanz-Hering

Around the year

Songs, activities and fun

with music compiled by Wolfgang E. Hering

Ernst Klett Sprachen
Stuttgart

Acknowledgements

p. 19 "The Wind" © James Reeves from *COMPLETE POEMS FOR CHILDREN* (FaberFinds). Reprinted by permission of the James Reeves Estate.

p. 19 "Rain" by Spike Milligan from Silly Verse for Kids. Reprinted by permission of Spike Milligan Productions Ltd, London.

p. 30 "The Ghosts of the Sea", original title: "Seegespenster" from *Komm, wir spielen.* © Fidula-Verlag Boppard/Rhein und Salzburg. www.fidula.eu

p. 108 "There are big waves" © Eleanor Farjeon from *BLACKBIRD HAS SPOKEN*. Macmillan. Reprinted by permission of David Higham Associates Ltd, London.

Every effort has been made to trace the copyright holders and we apologise in advance for any unintentional omissions. We will be pleased to make the necessary arrangements when *Around the year* is reprinted.

1st edition 8 7 6 5 4 | 2020 19 18 17 16

The last figure shown denotes the year of impression.

This is an updated version of *Around the year* (978-3-12-512741-8).

www.klett-sprachen.de

Author: Brigitte Schanz-Hering

Editor: Gilian Bathmaker
Project manager: Wolfgang Volz
Illustrations: Christa Janik, Stuttgart; Sven Palmowski, Barcelona
Illustration Cover: Matthias Pflügner
Cover and typesetting: Sandra Vrabec
Printing and binding: CEWE Stiftung & Co. KGaA, Germering
Printed in Germany

ISBN 978-3-12-512751-7

9 783125 127517

Introduction

Around the year has been produced for students in their first three years of learning English in secondary and in primary schools. It comprises a collection of lively and diverse supplementary material which includes songs, information, games and other activities all connected with festivals and events which take place throughout the year. The chapters are set in chronological order, except chapter 12, which is about birthdays and can therefore be used at any time of year. Each chapter relates to a specific time of year or event in the year, starting at the beginning and finishing at the end of the school year. Each chapter consists of two parts: (i) Teacher's notes, providing background information, suggestions for using the copy masters (worksheets) with solutions where applicable, and ideas for games and additional activities and (ii) copy masters.

It may well not be possible to use all the copy masters with any one class. Teachers should make individual choices which suit the needs and demands of their classes. Whatever the choice, *Around the year* aims to liven up English lessons as well as providing a valuable insight into British culture and traditions. The copy masters are intended to be copied and handed out to students. Students should keep all their handouts in a special folder. They can call this their "Around the year Album". They can also be encouraged to collect other relevant material from Britain or the USA in their folders, such as postcards, stickers, photos, etc. Many of the copy masters require students to cut things out and stick them in, to colour in pictures, and so on. It is therefore advisable to have the following things available in the classroom: scissors, coloured pencils or paints (or equivalent), glue, cardboard. Inevitably some of the vocabulary used in the copy masters and especially in the songs will be new to students. A dictionary/dictionaries should be available for quick reference and the teacher would be well-advised to introduce important new vocabulary (either via the overhead projector or blackboard) before working with a worksheet.

The songs on the CD have been recorded especially for the target group with varied and lively arrangements. The recordings provide an excellent means of introducing and teaching the songs as well as creating a special atmosphere in the classroom. Guitar chord diagrams of all the chords needed in the songs are given at the back of this book (page 111).

Many of the activities suggested are ideal for cross-curricular teaching: there are a number of recipes, which could be used in cookery lessons; many songs, which could be used in music lessons; many things to make and draw/paint, which could be used in art and craft lessons; there are even suggestions for activities which could be carried out as part of a nature (geography or biology) lesson. The songs are all easily identifiable by the CD symbol ◎. Other worksheets which are suitable for use in cross-curricular activities are marked ✱ in the list of contents.

Contents

Items marked * are suitable for use in cross-curricular teaching.
Items marked ◎ are on the CD which accompanies this book.

1 Back to School

The material in this chapter is intended for use at the very beginning of a new school year. The emphasis is on "warming up" to English (again), getting to know each other and talking about the holidays.

Inky Minky Tinky

This song has been specially written for the first day of term.
Start the song with the chorus which at the beginning is sung only half as fast as the rest of the song.
Then form five groups: one for each of the five verses of the song.
Each group sings their verse only. (Students could be asked to learn their verse by heart.)
Everybody sings the chorus. The chorus could also be sung by two groups, each singing alternate lines:

A: Inky minky tinky a booza dooza pinky
B: Ubba dubba dub dub doo.
A: Eeny meeny beeny oompah goompah jeany
B: Ubba dubba dub dub doo.

Remember to tell students to collect their handouts (see Introduction, page 7).

Games

Apples, Peaches

This is a choosing rhyme. It can be used to decide who should start a game, who is "it" in a game, who should be group leader, etc. (It can be used at any time of the year!)

1. The students stand/sit in a circle.
2. A student or the teacher points to each person in turn whilst saying:
   "Apples, peaches, pears, and plums,
   Tell me when your birthday comes."
3. The student pointed to on the word "comes" tells the others which month his/her birthday is in, e.g.: "May".
4. The "pointer" spells the month, pointing to one person for each letter, e. g. M – A – Y (one letter – one person).
5. The student pointed to on the last letter (here: "y") is "it".

Variation: Instead of spelling the name of the month the months leading up to the month can be chanted: e. g. "January – February – March – April – May". The student pointed to on the month (here: "May") is "it".

Catch the ball

For all these games you will need one or more small balls (e.g. tennis balls). Students and teacher start by sitting in a circle. The teacher has the ball.

I Introducing oneself

This game can be played with first names only or with first names and surnames. (If the students have been given English names, use these.)

Version 1

1. The teacher starts and gives his/her name: "My name's ..."/"I'm ..."
2. Then he/she throws the ball to one of the students asking: "(And) what's your name?"
3. The student catches the ball and calls out his/her name: "My name's ..."/"I'm ..."
4. The student throws the ball to another student and asks: "(And) what's your name?"
5. Repeat stages 3 and 4.

Version 2

1. The teacher throws the ball to student A and says: "Your name's. . ."/"You're. . ."
2. Student A catches the ball and stands up. The teacher takes the student's seat.
3. Student A throws the ball to student B saying "You're .../Your name's ..."
4. Now student A takes student B's seat and so on.

Variation: When students are familiar with the game have two or three students throwing balls. Use first names only.

II Talking about the holidays

Play this game as above, but here the teacher starts by talking about the holidays: "I spent my holidays in/at ..."/"I spent my holidays at home."/"I was on holiday in/at ..."/ "I was at home during the holidays." Then the teacher throws the ball to one of the students, who talks about his/her holidays, etc.

Variation: Student A throws the ball to student B and asks: "What did you do in your holidays?" Student B answers (e.g. "I went swimming almost every day"), throws the ball to student C and repeats the question, and so on.

Zip-Zap

1. Students and teacher sit in a circle except for one student who stands in the middle of the circle. This student is the caller.
2. The caller points at someone in the circle and says either "Zip", "Zap" or "Zip-Zap".
   Zip means: say the name of the person on your left.
   Zap means: say the name of the person on your right.
   Zip-Zap means: everybody change seats.
3. The person pointed at must respond appropriately, on Zip and Zap by saying: "His/her name is ..." On Zip- Zap everyone changes seats. The caller also tries to get a seat. The student left without a seat becomes the new caller.

Inky Minky Tinky

(words: Peter Ehlebracht/Robert Metcalf/Brigitte Schanz-Hering;
music: Peter Ehlebracht)

1. Today we all went back to school
   And something odd occurred:
   This morning when I woke
   My head was full of silly words – something like:

Chorus:

   Inky minky tinky a booza dooza pinky
   Ubba dubba dub dub doo.
   Eeny meeny beeny oompah goompah jeany
   Ubba dubba dub dub doo.

2. The words were all unknown to me –
   The meaning wasn't clear.
   But I just kept repeating them
   For everyone to hear – yes I sang:

   Chorus

3. I took the bus to go to school,
   And there sat my friend Lee.
   And suddenly he started singing
   Nonsense words to me – and he sang:

   Chorus

4. Now when the bus got to the school
   The two of us got out,
   And we were quite amazed to hear
   Our classmates sing and shout quite clearly:

   Chorus

5. The English teacher said to us:
   "To start this term off right,
   I'd like to teach you all
   Some brand-new words I learnt last night," –
   and he said:

   Chorus

ISBN 978-3-12-512751-7

2 Autumn, good morning! Summer, good night!

Autumn

Yellow the bracken,
Golden the sheaves,
Rosy the apples,
Crimson the leaves;
Mist on the hillsides,
Clouds grey and white.
Autumn, good morning!
Summer, good night!

(Florence Hoatson)

The activities in this section focus on autumn as harvest time and as a time of wet and windy weather.

World Harvest

2

Use the CD to introduce the song and tell the class that the song is about food from different countries. Ask the students to try to work out which countries the items of food come from. When the students are familiar with the song, divide the class into four groups. Each group sings one verse of the song. The chorus is sung by the whole class. One student could point out the countries on a map of the world as they are mentioned in the song. *World Harvest* could also be used when teaching topics such as shopping, food, countries/nationalities.

Food from different countries

3

This worksheet practises the names of the countries and food from the song *World Harvest* (copy master 2). It can also be used independently of the song.

Make it clear to the students that Africa is not a country, but a continent and that the official name for "Holland" is "The Netherlands".

Solution

1. Countries	Food	2. Where the food comes from
Africa	sardines	sardines – Portugal
Argentina	cheese	cheese – Holland
Brazil	grapes	grapes – France
China	currants	currants – Greece
France	coffee	coffee – Brazil
Greece	maize	maize – USA
Holland	bananas	bananas – Jamaica
India	beef	beef – Argentina
Italy	spices	spices – India
Jamaica	lemons	lemons – Italy
New Zealand	oranges	oranges – Spain
Portugal	rice	rice – China
Spain	butter	butter – New Zealand
USA	pineapples	pineapples – Africa

Fruit and vegetables: Painting by numbers

4

Students will need coloured pencils (or equivalent).
Make a transparency of the copy master. Introduce the new vocabulary via the overhead projector, first showing the pictures only, and then asking students to match the words with the right items.
Students can then be given their own copies of the worksheet to complete.

Fruit and vegetables: Word search

5

This worksheet provides further vocabulary practice.
Students can make use of the words in short dialogues:

A: "Do you like . . . ?" B: "Yes, I do/No, I don't. (I prefer ...)"
A: "What colour is/are . . . ?" B: "It's/They're ..."

Work in pairs or ask the class to make a question and answer chain: Student A asks student B who gives the answer and asks student C, and so on. When students are familiar with the chain, ask more than one student to start simultaneously.

Solution

apple	mushrooms
apricot	nut
bean	peach
carrots	pears
cauliflower	plums
celery	potatoes
cherry	rhubarb
grapes	strawberry
melon	tomatoes

M	E	L	O	N	F	E	D	T	G	V	H	U	F
U	A	G	N	D	S	Z	C	A	R	R	O	T	S
S	H	U	I	C	T	K	I	S	A	M	G	O	Z
H	X	V	O	W	R	Y	R	L	P	L	U	M	S
R	F	U	N	X	A	P	P	L	E	Y	B	A	D
O	L	T	S	A	W	P	E	F	S	N	L	T	O
O	G	E	H	C	B	E	A	N	M	P	S	O	R
M	O	T	P	U	E	W	C	X	Z	E	C	E	D
S	A	Y	A	K	R	I	N	F	M	A	O	S	C
E	L	B	P	B	R	H	U	B	A	R	B	G	E
C	H	E	R	R	Y	N	T	P	H	S	I	R	L
A	C	G	I	E	I	K	H	K	S	L	C	F	E
P	A	O	C	A	U	L	I	F	L	O	W	E	R
W	E	F	O	B	S	Y	N	A	D	T	X	R	Y
A	P	O	T	A	T	O	E	S	B	U	A	D	V

Mr Weatherman

6

The vocabulary in this song is quite difficult for students at this stage. Enough vocabulary should be explained before singing or listening to the song to allow gist understanding.

Introduce the song via the CD. It is then advisable for the teacher to sing the verses (or play the CD) and ask students to join in with the chorus only. When the last line of the chorus is sung students should draw a large sun in the air with their arms. In the last chorus the sun "rises" three times.

Students can draw pictures to illustrate each verse of the song as a kind of comprehension exercise. This could be done in six groups, two groups drawing a picture for each of the verses. The pictures (with the words below them) could then be used to decorate the classroom.

Weather Poems

7

Ask students to choose their favourite poem and learn it by heart.

Solution to riddle:

The wind.

Make your own windmill

8

The material required is listed on the worksheet. Either make the windmills in class, or ask students to make the windmills for homework. Encourage them to use dictionaries, but to try not to rely on you too much for help.

Autumn puzzles

9

These two puzzles are just for fun!

Solutions

1. I'm a kite.
2. The kite is on the end of string A

World Harvest

(chorus, melody and words: Richard Graves and Cecily Taylor;
verse melody: Jean Gilbert)

Chorus:

Push the trolley with the basket
Down between the rows of shelves.
See the tins and jars and packets,
This is how we serve ourselves.

1. First we sail to distant prairies
   Maize is ripening in the sun.
   Ready for our bowls of cornflakes
   When another day's begun.
   Let's steer on to warm Jamaica,
   Pick bananas from the trees,
   See the canes and get our sugar,
   Then sail on across the seas.

   Chorus

2. Next stop – beef from Argentina,
   Coffee beans – Brazil ahead!
   Round the world we find New Zealand,
   There's the butter for our bread.
   Now we travel on to China,
   Think of puddings made of rice;
   We'll collect some tea from India,
   Don't forget to find the spice.

   Chorus

3. Greece will have some dried sultanas,
   Currants, too, to fill our cakes,
   Pineapples from Africa and
   Lemons by Italian lakes.
   Tinned sardines in Portugal, and
   Juicy oranges from Spain,
   Grapes from France and cheese from Holland,
   Then we'll sail for home again.

   Chorus

4. Rosy apples in the orchards,
   New-laid eggs must not be missed,
   Vegetables from market gardens,
   Now we've ticked off all our list.
   Well, our trolley's really loaded,
   What a busy shopping day,
   Seems we needed all the world, and
   Now there's just the bill to pay.

   Chorus

ISBN 978-3-12-512751-7

Food from different countries

1. *What are the names of the countries and the different kinds of food?*
   The first letter of each word is underlined.

Countries		Food	
icArfa		nasdrise	
tAgninrea		esceeh	
liBzar		pregas	
hiCan		trucsran	
necraF		efocef	
cerGee		ziame	
dlanloH		sanaban	
dlnai		febe	
tylla		pecsis	
acamJai		solnem	
ewN/ aZdenla		gresona	
loPturag		erci	
napSi		trubet	
SUA		lepsiappne	

2. *The names of the countries and the different kinds of food do not go together. Work out where each kind of food comes from and write sentences.*

   Example: **Sardines come from Portugal.**

3. *Talk about the food you like/don't like with a partner. Use these phrases:*

ISBN 978-3-12-512751-7

Fruit and vegetables: Painting by numbers

1. *Colour the fruit and vegetables by numbers.*
2. *Write the correct letter next to the fruit and vegetables.*

- ◯ apple
- ◯ bananas
- ◯ cauliflower
- ◯ celery

- ◯ carrots
- ◯ gooseberry
- ◯ grapes
- ◯ mushrooms

- ◯ nuts
- ◯ pear
- ◯ peas
- ◯ plum

ISBN 978-3-12-512751-7

Fruit and vegetables: Word search

1. *Can you find the fruit and vegetables? The first one is done for you.*

M	E	L	O	N	F	E	D	T	G	V	H	U	F
U	A	G	N	D	S	Z	C	A	R	R	O	T	S
S	H	U	I	C	T	K	I	S	A	M	G	O	Z
H	X	V	O	W	R	Y	R	L	P	L	U	M	S
R	F	U	N	X	A	P	P	L	E	Y	B	A	D
O	L	T	S	A	W	P	E	F	S	N	L	T	O
O	G	E	H	C	B	E	A	N	M	P	S	O	R
M	O	T	P	U	E	W	C	X	Z	E	C	E	D
S	A	Y	A	K	R	I	N	F	M	A	O	S	C
E	L	B	P	B	R	H	U	B	A	R	B	G	E
C	H	E	R	R	Y	N	T	P	H	S	I	R	L
A	C	G	I	E	I	K	H	K	S	L	C	F	E
P	A	O	C	A	U	L	I	F	L	O	W	E	R
W	E	F	O	B	S	Y	N	A	D	T	X	R	Y
A	P	O	T	A	T	O	E	S	B	U	A	D	V

bean,

Score:

over 14 = excellent

11–14 = good

7–10 = fair

2. *What do you like? Can you make sentences?*

Example:

I like beans, but I don't like ...

ISBN 978-3-12-512751-7

Mr Weatherman

(words and music: Bernhard Hering/Wolfgang E. Hering/
Bernd Meyerholz; translation: A. Bowyer/B. Schanz-Hering)

1. When the weather's dark and dreary,
   And we're feeling sad and weary,
   Mr Weatherman, let your colours glow,
   Paint the sky with a big rainbow.
   When the rain beats on the window pane,
   And we think we'll never see the sun again,
   Mr Weatherman, do your stuff,
   Turn that great big rain tap off.

Chorus:

Dear Mr Weatherman,
Do what we know you can
Do what we know you can,
Do what we know you can.
Dear Mr Weatherman,
Do what we know you can,
Do what we know you can.
Let the sun come out!

2. When the playground's grey and wet,
   We're as bored as we can get,
   Mr Weatherman, with all your might –
   Warm the air up – we want to play outside.
   Cold winds have us in their grip,
   Make our eyes stream and noses drip,
   Mr Weatherman, do be nice,
   Send us your south wind to melt the ice.

Chorus

3. Now we see the lightning flash,
   All around us hear the thunder crash!
   Mr Weatherman, be quiet, please,
   We want to sleep and get some peace!
   Turn your sun lamp right up high,
   Clear those grey clouds out of the sky,
   Blow the fog and drizzle away,
   We'd like to have a sunny day.

Chorus

ISBN 978-3-12-512751-7

Weather Poems

A tongue twister

Whether the weather be fine, or whether the weather be not,
Whether the weather be cold, or whether the weather be hot,
We'll weather the weather, whatever the weather,
Whether we like it or not.

Who am I?

I can get through a doorway without any key,
And strip the leaves from the great oak tree.

(James Reeves)

A limerick

There was a young lady from Spain
Who couldn't go out in the rain,
Cause she'd lent her umbrella
To Queen Isabella,
Who never returned it again.

Doctor Foster

Doctor Foster went to Gloucester
In a shower of rain;
He stepped in a puddle,
Right up to his middle,
And never went there again.

Rain

There are holes in the sky
Where the rain gets in.
But they're ever so small
That's why rain is thin.

(Spike Milligan)

ISBN 978-3-12-512751-7

Make your own windmill

You will need:

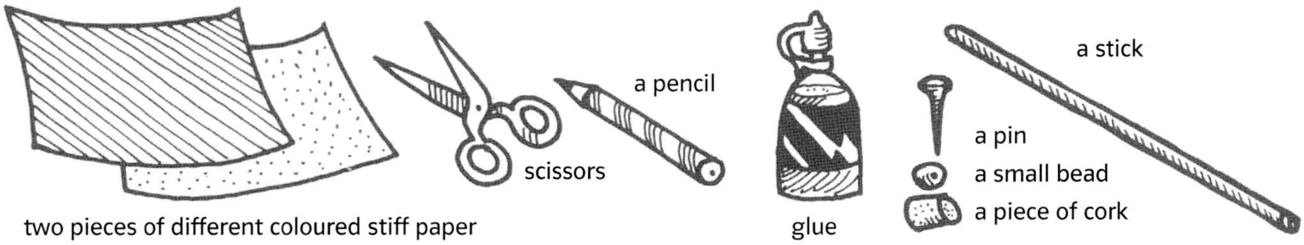

1. *Draw a square about 20 cm by 20 cm on each piece of paper.*

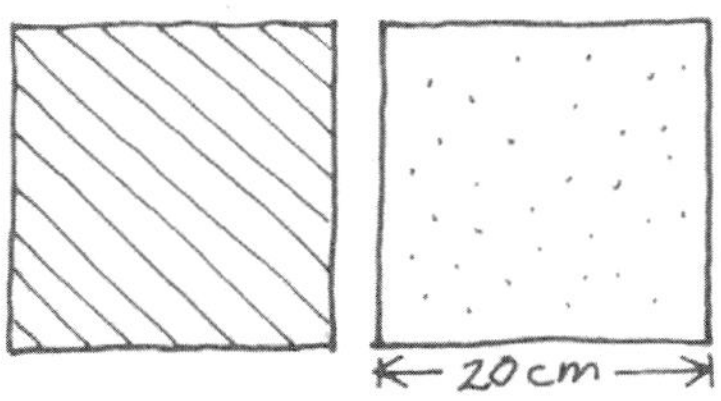

2. *Cut the squares out and stick them together.*

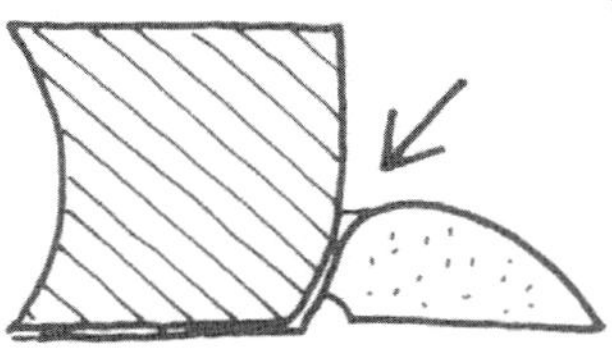

3. *Draw lines from corner to corner.*

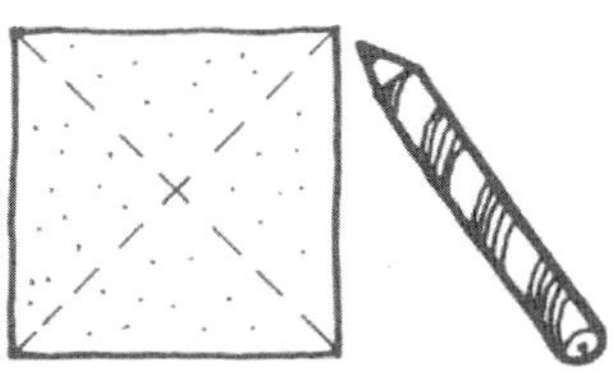

4. *Cut along the lines. Stop 3 cm from the centre.*

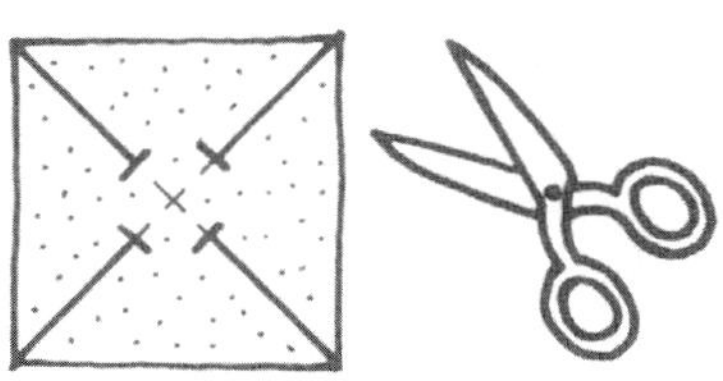

5. *Fold each corner into the centre. Now secure it with the pin.*

6. *Thread the bead onto the pin. (If there is not a bead or some space between the stick and the windmill it will not turn round.)*

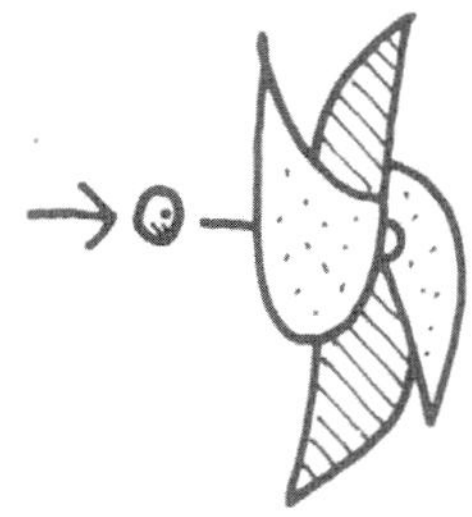

7. *Stick the pin into the end of the stick.*

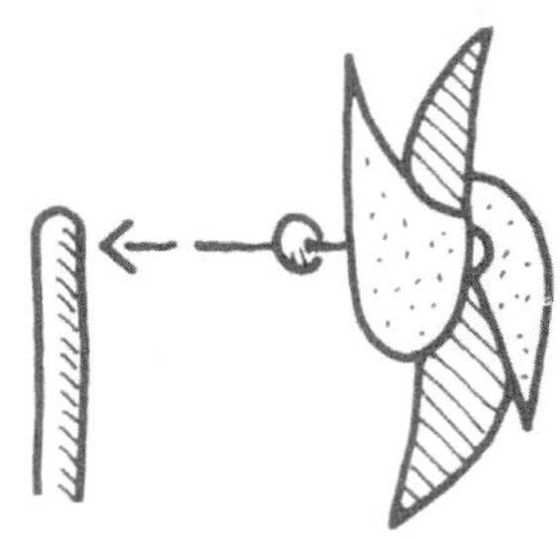

8. *If the point of the pin comes out of the back of the stick, push the piece of cork into it.*

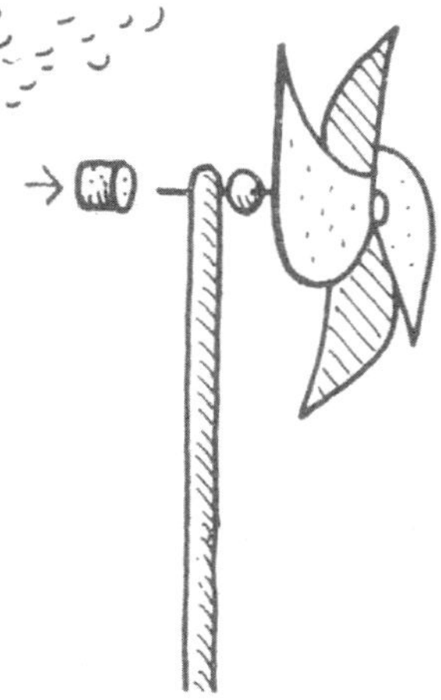

ISBN 978-3-12-512751-7

Autumn puzzles

1. *Join the dots. What am I?*

2. *Which piece of string is the kite tied on to?*

ISBN 978-3-12-512751-7

3 Witches, ghosts and bonfires

These worksheets and activities should be carried out around the end of October and the beginning of November, at the time when Halloween and Guy Fawkes Night are celebrated.

Witch Watch

10

Witch Watch can be sung as a call and response song. Divide the class into two groups, A and B, and sing the lines of the verses as follows:

A: lines 1 and 4
B: lines 2 and 5
A+B: lines 3 and 6

Example:

Verse 1
A: It's the witch, witch, witches
B: That watch, watch, watch
A+B: Until you go to bed.
A: Then they zoom, zoom, zoom
B: On their broom, broom, brooms,
A+B: Right above your head.

The chorus is sung as follows:
A: Fly witch,
B: fly high,
A+B: Right above our heads.
A: Fly witch,
B: fly high,
A+B: While we dream in bed.

Variation: As witches come at night they use very low voices. Sing the song in whispers.

Halloween (31st October)

11

Some information about Halloween, which could be copied and given to more able students, is given on page 23. The teacher should make a copy of the worksheet onto a transparency or scan it and present it via whiteboard or computer and beamer. While presenting the information to students (possibly in their mother tongue) the teacher can then teach and practise the new words before students are given the worksheet to do themselves.
There are also two Halloween poems on the worksheet, *Jack-o'-lantern* and *Dark*. *Jack-o'-lantern* is an action poem. Ask students to make up actions of their own to go with the text. Alternatively, tell them to make the following actions:

Text	**Actions**
I am a pumpkin, big and round.	Make a circle above the head with the arms.
Once upon a time, I grew on the ground.	Point to the ground.
Now I have a mouth, two eyes and a nose.	Touch mouth, eyes, and nose.
What are they for, do you suppose?	Scratch head as if asking a question.
With a candle inside,	Raise one arm.
Shining bright,	Both arms make a circle in front of body.
I'll be a jack-o'-lantern on Halloween night.	Make a horrible face using the hands for extra effect.

Dark can be read by the teacher and/or students in a deep, low voice. All except the last word ("ghost"), that is, which should be shouted out as a cry!

Halloween

Halloween is the 31st October. A very long time ago (in Celtic times) the festivals at this time of year marked the beginning of the New Year: it was the end of summer and the beginning of winter. People wore masks and made fires to frighten away the evil spirits. Today you can still see witches and ghosts at Halloween – but usually they are just young people who have dressed up to go to Halloween parties. At these parties you play games like apple-bobbing: you have to get apples out of a bowl of water using only your teeth! The big, ugly faces you might see in windows or doorways are "jack-o'-lanterns". They are hollowed-out pumpkins with faces cut out of them and a candle inside. *(See poem on copy master 11).* The lanterns are also supposed to frighten away witches and ghosts! If the doorbell rings on Halloween it's probably some young children playing "trick or treat". Give them a treat (some sweets or money) and they will go away and leave you in peace. But give them nothing and they will play a trick on you, like putting a dead mouse on your doorstep or bad eggs through your letter-box. (The tradition of "trick or treating" is much more widespread in the USA, where it has also reached much more drastic proportions: "tricks" are no longer always just harmless fun. Some tricks involve dangerous and violent activities, where much damage is caused.)

Due to commercial reasons it has become popular to celebrate Halloween all over the world. Thus it is even more important to give students ideas about the roots.

Game

Apple-bobbing

Have an apple-bobbing competition in class. Ask each student to bring three apples with them.

1. Float 6 apples in a bowl of water on the floor.
2. Two students kneel down on either side of the bowl with their hands behind their backs.
3. When the teacher or another student says "go" the students must try to get three apples out of the water using their teeth only.
4. The first to get three apples out is the winner. (You could time the students and find the class champion!)

Colour the witch

Students will need coloured pencils (or equivalent), scissors, glue and sticky tape. The finished witches can be taped to the classroom window. Two or more witches can be made into a mobile and hung up in the classroom.

12

The Ghosts of the Sea

13

This is an action song. The students can accompany the song from the beginning by pretending to be "waves": they clap in time to the music (i. e. on the first beat of every bar) once to the right-hand side and once to the left for each line of the verses.
There is no clapping during the chorus. Now "the ghosts of the sea" appear. The students make the tocking sound by hitting their right fists onto their left palms. Then they hiss: "Sssssss. . ." and wiggle their fingers. On "Oooooooagh" they pretend to be ghosts by waving their arms in a scary way and uttering little screams. While the last two lines of the chorus are sung everybody should remain still and quiet before starting to clap to the next verse again.

Variation: Role-play
Students can act out the scenes in the verses. The following characters appear: watchman, cook, captain, ghost, crew. They can act the scenes while other students sing the song. Some students could dress up as ghosts and appear during the chorus.

Variation: Sounds orchestra
Instead of singing, one or two students could read out the text of the song. A "sounds orchestra" can then make the "music": roaring sea, snoring crew, tolling bell, howling wind, groaning, rustling and creaking ghosts, screaming cook. The scenes can be mimed at the same time.

Game

Vampires
This is an ideal game for occasions like Halloween. It can, of course, be played on other occasions, too, such as at Carnival time.

1. Students walk around the classroom with their eyes closed. Ideally the classroom should be completely darkened.
2. The teacher whispers to one student that he/she is a vampire.
3. The vampire, still with the eyes closed, now tries to find a "victim".
4. When the vampire meets another student it takes his/her hand and gives it a gentle squeeze. The victim utters a sharp cry and becomes a vampire, too.
5. Now the two vampires try to find new victims and so the number of vampires increases.
6. If one vampire meets and touches another one, both of them become "human beings" again. Vampires don't cry when being squeezed.

Guy Fawkes Night (November 5th)

14

Some information about Guy Fawkes Night, which could be copied and given to more able students, is given below. The teacher should present this information to students (possibly in their mother tongue) as well as the new vocabulary (see worksheet) before asking students to complete the tasks.
In addition to the cloze text, which is a kind of comprehension exercise, there is a maze – for fun, and a famous poem, which is known by heart by almost all children/people in Britain. The poem very briefly explains why November 5th is celebrated. The vocabulary in the poem will need to be explained first.

Guy Fawkes Night

In 1605 a gang of Catholic men made a plan (or plot – *see poem on copy master 14*) to kill the King, James I. Guy Fawkes was a member of the gang.
The gang wanted England to be Catholic but although James I was a Catholic himself, England remained Protestant.
The gang knew that King James was going to the Houses of Parliament in London on November 5th, and that all the other members of Parliament would be there, too. So they decided to use gunpowder and blow up the Houses of Parliament when the King was there. The plan failed because one member of the gang sent a letter to one of his relatives warning him not to go to Parliament on that day. The police searched the House the night before November 5th. Guy Fawkes was arrested and later hanged for treason: trying to kill the king. The rest of the gang escaped, but were killed soon after in a fight. It is this failed attempt to kill the King which is remembered to this day, although the history behind the event is now no longer of such great importance! Today November 5th – or Guy Fawkes Night, or simply Bonfire Night – is when people in Britain let off fireworks and have large bonfires. Some children make "guys" out of old clothes stuffed with newspapers and straw and with masks for faces. They take them on the streets in the days leading up to Bonfire Night and call out: "Penny for the guy", in the hope of getting money from passers-by. On Bonfire Night the guys are burnt on top of the bonfires!
Unfortunately there have been many accidents and even people killed when setting off fireworks or playing near bonfires at private parties. Children under 14 are not allowed to buy fireworks. And now most towns organise a big Bonfire Night celebration for all the people, with a huge bonfire, an impressive firework display and, of course, things to eat and drink, like hot baked potatoes, sausages and soup! In Britain this is the only night in the year when fireworks are let off: there are no fireworks at New Year, for example.

I like the fireworks

15

This song can be sung in two groups or as a round in four parts.
Divide the class into two groups, A and B.
Group A sings the last two lines of the first verse throughout the song:

"Boom-de-ah-da, boom-de-ah-da,
Boom-de-ah-da, boom-de-ah-ay."

Group B sings the actual verses.
Both groups sing the last two (in the second verse three) lines of the verses together.
To sing as a round, divide the class into four groups. Use only one verse. First everyone sings the verse. Then each new part comes in every two bars (i. e. when the previous group has sung the first two lines). When the teacher gives a sign everybody sings the ending: "Boom, boom, boom."

Variation: It is possible to sing the song as a round using both verses. The two verses must be sung directly one after the other without a pause.

16

Draw an Autumn Picture

Students will need coloured pencils (or equivalent).
This worksheet is intended as a kind of comprehension exercise in which students can show that they are familiar with autumn vocabulary. This exercise is repeated at the end of each season. There is a gap in the heading of the copy master so you can use it for every season.
First have the students complete the heading of the picture, then give the students the following instructions. Before or while you read out the instructions, you may write the important vocabulary on the blackboard or overhead projector.

Draw an autumn picture and colour it in. Draw
- a child flying a kite and another one holding a windmill on the right-hand side of the river;
- a ghost in the bottom right-hand corner of the picture;
- a witch stirring a pot and her cat on the hill on the right;
- a pumpkin face in one window of the house;
- smoke coming out of the chimney of the house;
- a tree with its leaves falling on the left-hand side of the house;
- a basket with freshly picked apples under the tree;
- a bonfire on the right-hand side of the house;
- dark clouds in the sky;
- rain falling.

Witch Watch

(words and music: Jane Morgan)

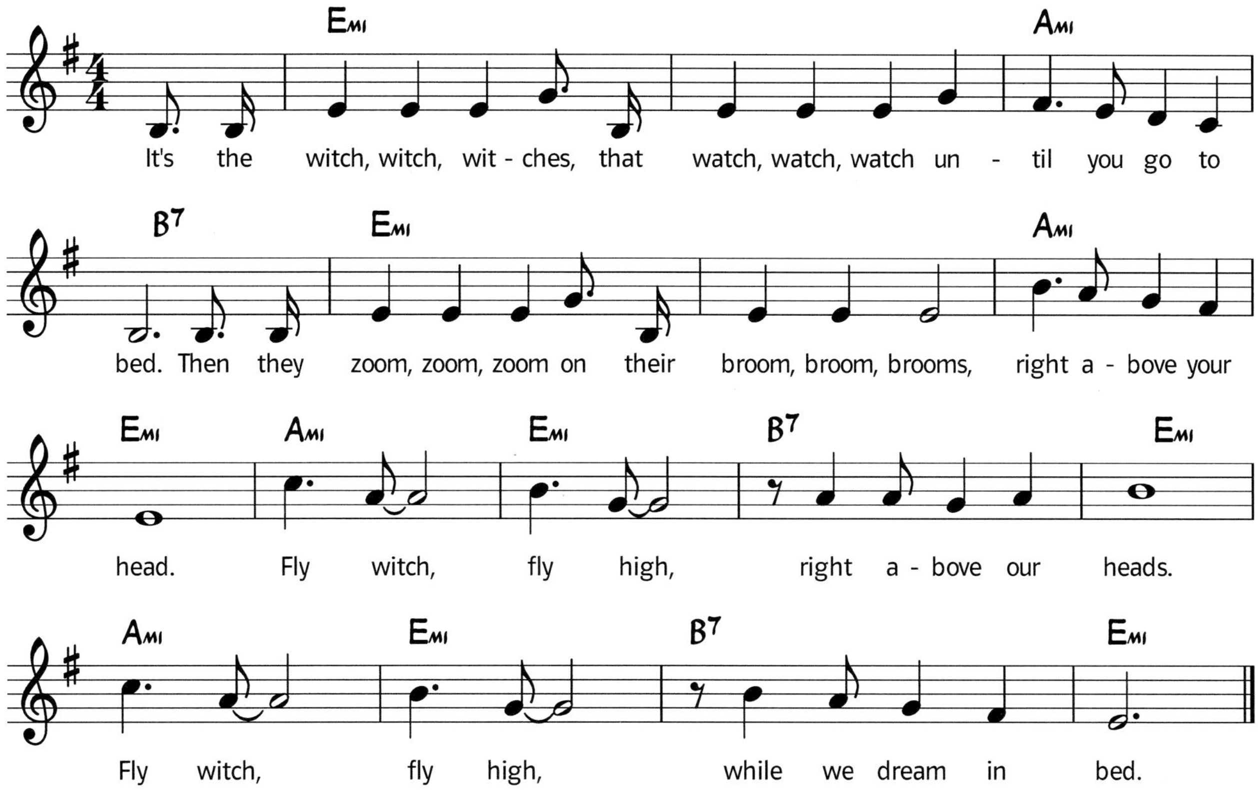

1. It's the witch, witch, witches
   That watch, watch, watch
   Until you go to bed.
   Then they zoom, zoom, zoom
   On their broom, broom, brooms,
   Right above your head.

Chorus:

Fly witch, fly high,
Right above our heads.
Fly witch, fly high,
While we dream in bed.

2. Then the witch, witch, witches
   That watch, watch, watch,
   Fly down to make their spells.
   Hear them whirr, whirr, whirr,
   See them stir, stir, stir,
   There in caves and dells.

   Chorus

3. See their tall, black hats,
   See their slinky cats,
   These witches of the night.
   See them twist and turn,
   See them cook and churn,
   Misty, magic sight.

   Chorus

ISBN 978-3-12-512751-7

Halloween

Jack-o'-lantern

I am a pumpkin, big and round.
Once upon a time I grew on the ground.
Now I have a mouth, two eyes and a nose.
What are they for do you suppose?
With a candle inside, shining bright,
I'll be a jack-o'-lantern on Halloween night.

Dark

In the dark, dark, wood, there was a dark, dark house.
And in that dark, dark house, there was a dark, dark room.
And in that dark, dark room, there was a dark, dark shelf.
And on that dark, dark shelf, there was a dark, dark box.
And in that dark, dark box, there was a GHOST!

(Anonymous)

1. What do you know about Halloween in Britain? Write the words next to the right pictures. Then you can colour the pictures in or draw your own Halloween picture – perhaps to go with one of the poems.

witch • ghosts • apple-bobbing • pumpkin • masks • broomstick • Trick or treat • fancy dress party • jack-o'-lantern

2. Can you finish the sentences using the words?

The 31st October in Britain is called Halloween. In the evening many people go to ___ ___ ___ ___ ___ / ___ ___ ___ ___ ___ parties. They dress up as ___ ___ ___ ___ ___ ___ ___ and ___ ___ ___ ___ ___ ___ . At the parties young people play games like ___ ___ ___ ___ ___ - ___ ___ ___ ___ ___ ___ ___ . Children knock on doors and say: "___ ___ ___ ___ ___ / ___ ___ / ___ ___ ___ ___ ___ ?" People cut faces in ___ ___ ___ ___ ___ ___ ___ s. They put candles in them and put them in the windows of their houses. They are called ___ ___ ___ ___ -___ - ___ ___ ___ ___ ___ ___ ___ s.

ISBN 978-3-12-512751-7

Colour the witch

1. *Colour both witches.*
2. *Stick them together back to back.*
3. *Tape your witch to a window or make a mobile by hanging your witch with some others from the ceiling.*

The little witches
One little, two little, three little witches
Fly over haystacks, fly over ditches,
Slide down moonbeams without any britches –
Heigh ho, Halloween's here!

ISBN 978-3-12-512751-7

The Ghosts of the Sea

(words and music: Bernhard Hering/Wolfgang E. Hering/Bernd Meyerholz;
translation: Andy Bowyer/Robert Metcalf/Brigitte Schanz-Hering)

1. A ship is sailing on the sea,
   A bell begins to toll;
   The second mate's on watch tonight,
   The mighty waters roll.
   The crew are sleeping in their bunks;
   What is this eerie light?
   A greenish something on the bow –
   Which echoes in the night.

Chorus:
   It goes: tock, tock, tock, tock, tock, tock, tock,
   And hisses: ssssss ... and
   Suddenly it goes: oooooooagh!
   But don't go looking for the ghosts,
   You won't see where they are.

2. The cook is dreaming of the girl
   He left back at the Cape.
   He's woken by a groaning noise,
   And thinks he sees a shape.
   And with a scream, his hair on end
   He leaps out of his bed;
   A voice says, "Don't make such a din –
   D'you want to wake the dead?"

Chorus

3. The captain and his daring crew,
   Are standing now agape;
   Another ghost has just appeared,
   Of quite a frightening shape.
   The ship goes up, the ship goes down,
   The captain with a frown,
   Says, "Lads, I bid you all farewell;
   I fear we all shall drown".

Chorus

4. Then all at once the sea is calm,
   The sky begins to clear,
   The ghosts appear at the door,
   The crew are struck with fear
   "We're sorry, but you're much too loud,
   This wailing must now cease;
   We're going to find another ship,
   We want to rest in peace."

Chorus

ISBN 978-3-12-512751-7

Guy Fawkes Night

Remember, remember the fifth of November,
Gunpowder, treason and plot;
I see no reason why gunpowder treason
Should ever be forgot.

What happens on Guy Fawkes Night in Britain?
Choose the right words from the box and finish the sentences.

Guy Fawkes Night • fireworks • money • bonfires • guys • November • Bonfire Night • Penny for the guy!

In Britain _ _ _ _ _ _ _ _ 5th is called _ _ _ / _ _ _ _ _ _ / _ _ _ _ _

or _ _ _ _ _ _ _ / _ _ _ _ _ .

People have big _ _ _ _ _ _ _ _ .

They let off _ _ _ _ _ _ _ _ _ . Children make _ _ _ _ out of old clothes stuffed with straw and newspaper. They stand in the streets with their guys and say: "_ _ _ _ _ / _ _ _ / _ _ _ / _ _ _".

If they are lucky people give them _ _ _ _ _ . Later they put the guys on top of the big bonfires and burn them!

Bonfire Maze

Find the way to the guy's hat.
Start here.

ISBN 978-3-12-512751-7

I like the fireworks

(words: Wolfgang E. Hering/Brigitte Schanz-Hering; music: trad.)

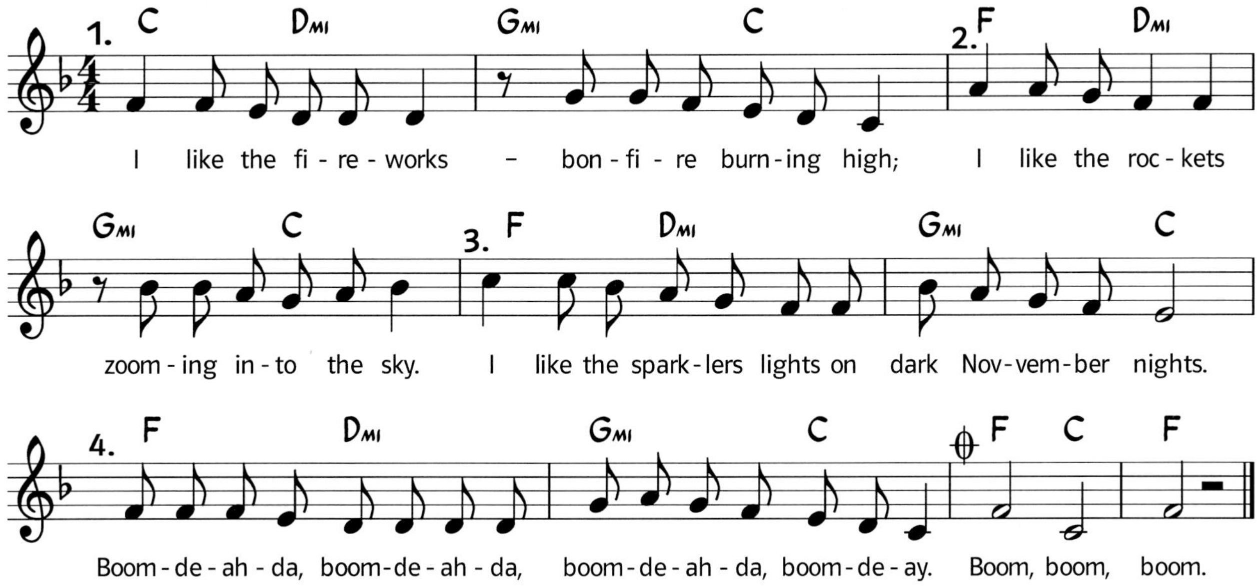

1. I like the fireworks –
   Bonfire burning high;
   I like the rockets
   Zooming into the sky.
   I like the sparklers' lights
   On dark November nights.
   Boom-de-ah-da, boom-de-ah-da,
   Boom-de-ah-da, boom-de-ay.

2. I like the Catherine wheels
   Whirling brightly round and round.
   I like the crackers,
   Bang – can't you hear their sound?
   I like the Bengal lights
   On dark November nights.
   Boom-de-ah-da, boom-de-ah-da,
   Boom-de-ah-da, boom-de-ay.

   Boom, boom, boom.

ISBN 978-3-12-512751-7
Klett

Draw ________ Picture

ISBN 978-3-12-512751-7

4 Merry Christmas!

These activities give an insight into the way Christmas is celebrated in Britain.

We wish you a merry Christmas

17

This is probably the most famous Christmas song of all. It should be sung in a lively, happy way. Traditionally it is sung by carol singers before they have been "paid" and move on to a new house. (Hence, "We won't go until we've got some.")

Merry Christmas!

18

Students will need coloured pencils (or equivalent).
The most important information and vocabulary relevant to Christmas in Britain can be found on this worksheet. Some information about Christmas in Britain, which could be copied and given to more able students, is given below. The teacher should make a copy of the worksheet onto a transparency and present it to students via the overhead projector. While giving the information below (possibly in the mother tongue) the teacher can then point out the various items and practise the new vocabulary.
When students are given their own copies of the worksheet ask them to colour them in and make them look really "Christmassy".

Christmas in Britain

(The words printed in **bold** type are featured on copy master 18.)
The first sign that Christmas is on its way is when you see **Christmas cards** on sale in the shops. This is usually in late September! Things which are often shown on cards are **robins**, **holly**, **Father Christmas**'s and jolly Christmas scenes. (Religious scenes are less common.) In Britain people buy and send great numbers of Christmas cards. They often buy them early, but they don't actually send them until the beginning of December! People put the cards they get on the **mantlepiece** over the fire in their sitting rooms, or hang them on the walls on pieces of coloured string.
About ten days before Christmas many people decorate their houses. They hang up brightly coloured balloons, paper chains, paper lanterns and other **decorations**. Most people have a **Christmas tree** in their sitting room. They decorate it with **tinsel**, **baubles**, chocolate and small coloured lights called "**fairy lights**", and on the top of the tree they put a **fairy** (or sometimes a star).
Carol singers go round the streets from house to house in the days leading up to Christmas. They sing carols and collect money for charity.
Holly and **mistletoe** are also typical of Christmas in Britain. People make **wreaths** out of holly and hang them on their front doors. They hang mistletoe from the ceiling and if two people meet under the mistletoe they can/must **kiss** each other!
In the theatres around Britain there are many pantomimes before Christmas. These are plays usually based on well-known children's stories or nursery rhymes. They are always funny, and always involve the audience by making them call out things, for example, "boo" when a bad character walks on to the stage!
The 24th December is called **Christmas Eve**. **Christmas Eve** is the night for having a lot of fun! Parents often take young children to an afternoon pantomime

performance. Others go to special shows at the theatre. Young people have **parties** with lots of singing and dancing. But you don't get your presents on Christmas Eve! The story is, that Father Christmas (or Santa Claus) flies through the sky on Christmas Eve in a **sleigh** pulled by **reindeer**. He delivers the presents while everyone is asleep. He comes down the **chimney** and puts the presents into **stockings** which have been hung up for him!

The 25th December is **Christmas Day**. People open their presents in the morning and then get ready for a big traditional **Christmas Dinner** of **roast turkey**, **roast potatoes**, **Brussels sprouts** and many other vegetables. At the table people pull **crackers**, which have **paper hats**, a **joke** and a small **gift** inside them. Families wear the paper hats at the dinner table! For dessert they eat **Christmas pudding** (a rich fruit mixture, which is made up to two months before Christmas and steamed for two or three hours on Christmas Day), or **mince pies** and cream, or trifle (see copy master 22). Later there is Christmas cake: a rich fruit cake covered in marzipan and thick white icing.

There are usually very good films and programmes on TV at Christmas. And at 3 o'clock on Christmas Day there is the **Queen's Speech**, in which the Queen talks about the past year and wishes everyone a happy Christmas.

The 26th December is called **Boxing Day**. In the past rich people used to give presents to their servants in boxes on this day. Nowadays people spend Boxing Day relaxing or visiting friends and relatives.

Further activities

Making a Christmas card

Students will need stiff paper and coloured pencils (or equivalent).

Ask students to make their own English Christmas cards. Tell them to use the illustrations on copy master 18 for ideas as well as the information they have been given. They could make their cards even more extravagant by decorating them with glitter and tinsel. Tell them to put the following text inside their cards:

To *Diana*
Merry Christmas and a Happy New Year!
With love from
Charles

A quiz

You can ask the students to do this quiz individually, but it is more fun to play it as a team game. Questions and answers are on page 36. You could ask the questions (and accept answers) in the mother tongue. The questions can be asked in any order. You can also make up your own questions, of course. You will need a small bell, a tambourine, and a gong (or similar instruments).

1. Divide the class into two or three teams.
2. Assign one instrument to each team.
3. The teams line up at the back of the classroom.
4. The instruments are put on a table at the front of the classroom in front of each team.

5. Ask a question. The first person in the team works out the answer (he/she may use copy master 18 and ask other members of the team for help), then runs to the front and makes a noise with the instrument.
6. The first one to sound their instrument can answer the question. If the answer is correct, the team gets one point. If the answer is wrong, the other teams get a point and the teacher gives the correct answer.
7. Members of teams take it in turns to run to the front.
8. The team with the most points at the end is the winner.

Questions	Answers
1. What do English people put on top of their Christmas trees?	*A fairy or sometimes a star*
2. When do English people open their Christmas presents?	*25th December/Christmas Day*
3. What do the English call 25th December?	*Christmas Day*
4. What do the English call 24th December?	*Christmas Eve*
5. When is Boxing Day?	*26th December*
6. Who is on TV at 3 pm on Christmas Day?	*The Queen*
7. What can/must you do under the mistletoe?	*Kiss*
8. What do English people have for dinner on Christmas Day?	*Roast turkey, roast potatoes, Brussels sprouts*
9. What do they have for dessert?	*Christmas pudding, mince pies or trifle*
10. What do the English often do on Christmas Eve?	*Have parties, go to the theatre*
11. What do you get inside a cracker?	*A joke, a hat and a small gift*
12. What do English people make wreaths out of?	*Holly*
13. How does Father Christmas get into people's houses?	*Through the chimney*
14. What does Father Christmas ride in?	*A sleigh pulled by reindeer*
15. What does Father Christmas put the presents in?	*A stocking*
16. Where do people put their Christmas cards?	*On the mantlepiece, on the wall*
17. What is the other name for Father Christmas?	*Santa Claus*
18. Which bird do you see on many Christmas cards?	*A robin*
19. What do English people decorate their Christmas trees with?	*Tinsel, baubles and fairy lights*
20. What do you call the people who go round singing at people's doors at Christmas?	*Carol singers*

Christmas Bingo

19 & 20

Copy master 19 is a set of word cards, copy master 20 provides the corresponding picture cards. It is advisable to make the cards more durable by sticking the copies onto cardboard before cutting them out. (Students could be asked to do this.)

Before starting to play make sure that the students are familiar with the vocabulary on the word cards. Pronounciation should be practised thoroughly, so that students do not have too much difficulty understanding one another.

1. Divide the class into groups of four to six.
2. Each group will need one set of word cards and two sets of picture cards.
3. One member of each group is appointed "caller". The caller does not take part in the round.
4. The caller shuffles the word cards and places them face down in a pile (A) in front of him/her.
5. The picture cards are spread out face up and each player takes it in turn to take one card until they each have six different pictures. Each player places the six cards in front of her/him on the table. Any remaining cards can be put to one side.
6. The caller takes the top word card from pile (A), reads it out and then places it face down on a new pile (B) on the table.
7. If a player has the corresponding picture card she/he can turn it over.
8. As soon as one of the players has turned over all six of her/his picture cards she/he calls out "BINGO" and is the winner of the game. The caller can check that the player really has won by matching the player's picture cards with word cards from pile (B).
9. The winner becomes the caller in the next round. The players take new picture cards in each new round.

Variation: Play the game as a class instead of in groups. You will need one set of word cards and enough picture cards for each student to have six different pictures. In the first round the teacher can be the caller.

Colour the Christmas tree

21

Students will need coloured pencils (or equivalent).
This worksheet practises and introduces some more Christmas vocabulary as well as practising colours. Use the finished pictures to decorate the classroom and create a Christmas atmosphere!

A Recipe: Trifle

22

Trifle is traditionally served as an alternative to Christmas pudding after Christmas Dinner. Often the sponge biscuits are soaked in sherry to make a sherry trifle. The ingredients needed are given on the worksheet. (Custard is a vanilla-flavoured sauce made with milk, eggs, sugar and vanilla flavouring. It becomes solid when cold, as does jelly, which is a fruit-flavoured gelatine mixture. Both jelly and custard are easily available in most countries in packet form.)

Mary's boy-child

23

This carol is actually from the West Indies which is illustrated in the sometimes rather odd-sounding language and grammar! It is quite a well-known Christmas song and was made famous as a hit record.

We wish you a merry Christmas

(words and music: traditional English)

1. We wish you a merry Christmas,
   We wish you a merry Christmas,
   We wish you a merry Christmas,
   And a happy New Year.

Chorus:

Good tidings we bring
To you and your kin,
We wish you a merry Christmas,
And a happy New Year.

2. Now bring us some Christmas pudding,
   Now bring us some Christmas pudding,
   Now bring us some Christmas pudding,
   And bring us some here.

Chorus

3. We won't go until we've got some,
   We won't go until we've got some,
   We won't go until we've got some,
   So bring some right here.

Chorus

4. For we all like Christmas pudding,
   For we all like Christmas pudding,
   For we all like Christmas pudding,
   So bring some out here.

Chorus

ISBN 978-3-12-512751-7

Merry Christmas!

ISBN 978-3-12-512751-7

Christmas Bingo: Word Cards

Christmas tree	Santa Claus	Christmas carol	Christmas Eve
Christmas Day	Father Christmas	Boxing Day	sleigh
reindeer	Christmas card	Christmas dinner	Christmas cake
Christmas pudding	decorations	holly	mistletoe
tinsel	December	snow	candles
stockings	turkey	toys	presents
games	Merry Christmas!	chimney	sweets
fairy	chocolate	mince pies	fruit
winter	apples	oranges	stars
robin	snowman	cracker	carol singers

ISBN 978-3-12-512751-7

Christmas Bingo: Picture cards

ISBN 978-3-12-512751-7

Colour the Christmas tree

Colour

- the Christmas tree: dark green
- Santa Claus' hat: red with white fur
- Santa Claus' beard: white
- Santa Claus' coat: red
- Santa Claus' belt and boots: black
- the trumpet: silver (grey)
- the tinsel: red
- the house: blue with a white roof and yellow door
- the balls: orange
- the bird: light green
- the apples: red
- the pears: yellow
- the sticks: red and white
- the bells: pink
- the pine cones: dark brown
- the gingerbread man: light brown
- the fish: violet
- the star: yellow
- the presents: any colours you like

ISBN 978-3-12-512751-7

A Recipe: Trifle

Trifle is a cold fruity dessert which has three (or sometimes even more) layers. At Christmas in Britain people often eat trifle as well as Christmas pudding and mince pies after their Christmas dinner. Trifle is easy to make. You often have trifle as a dessert at other times of the year, too, at birthday parties, for example.

You will need:

150 g sponge fingers
1 small tin mandarin oranges
1 banana
1 (or 2) packet(s) of jelly (to make with 1/2 litre of water)
1 (or 2) packet(s) of custard (to make with 1/2 litre of milk)
1/2 litre water
1/2 litre milk
1 cartoon cream
grated chocolate to decorate

A deep glass dish about 26 cms in diameter and at least 10 cms deep.

1. Drain the mandarin oranges but keep the juice.
2. Peel the banana and then slice it thinly.
3. Arrange the fruit and the sponge fingers in the bottom of the dish.
4. Make the jelly following the instructions on the packet. Use the juice from the oranges as well as water.
5. Allow the jelly to cool a little, then pour it over the fruit and sponge fingers. Put the dish in the fridge to cool. Leave it for at least half an hour. Now you have one layer!
6. Make the custard following the instructions on the packet.
7. Allow the custard to cool and then pour it into the dish on top of the jelly mixture. Put the dish in the fridge for at least an hour. Now you have two layers!
8. Whip the cream until it is very stiff.
9. When the custard is cold and has set (after at least one hour), spread the cream on the top. Now you have all three layers!
10. You can make a pattern on top of the cream using a fork, then sprinkle chocolate over the top.

Keep the trifle in the fridge. It keeps for about three days.

Variation: You can also use different kinds of tinned or fresh fruit.
You can decorate the top of the trifle with pieces of fruit, nuts, etc.
You can make small individual trifles in small dishes for each of the guests at a party.

ISBN 978-3-12-512751-7

Mary's boy-child

(words and music: Jester Hairston)

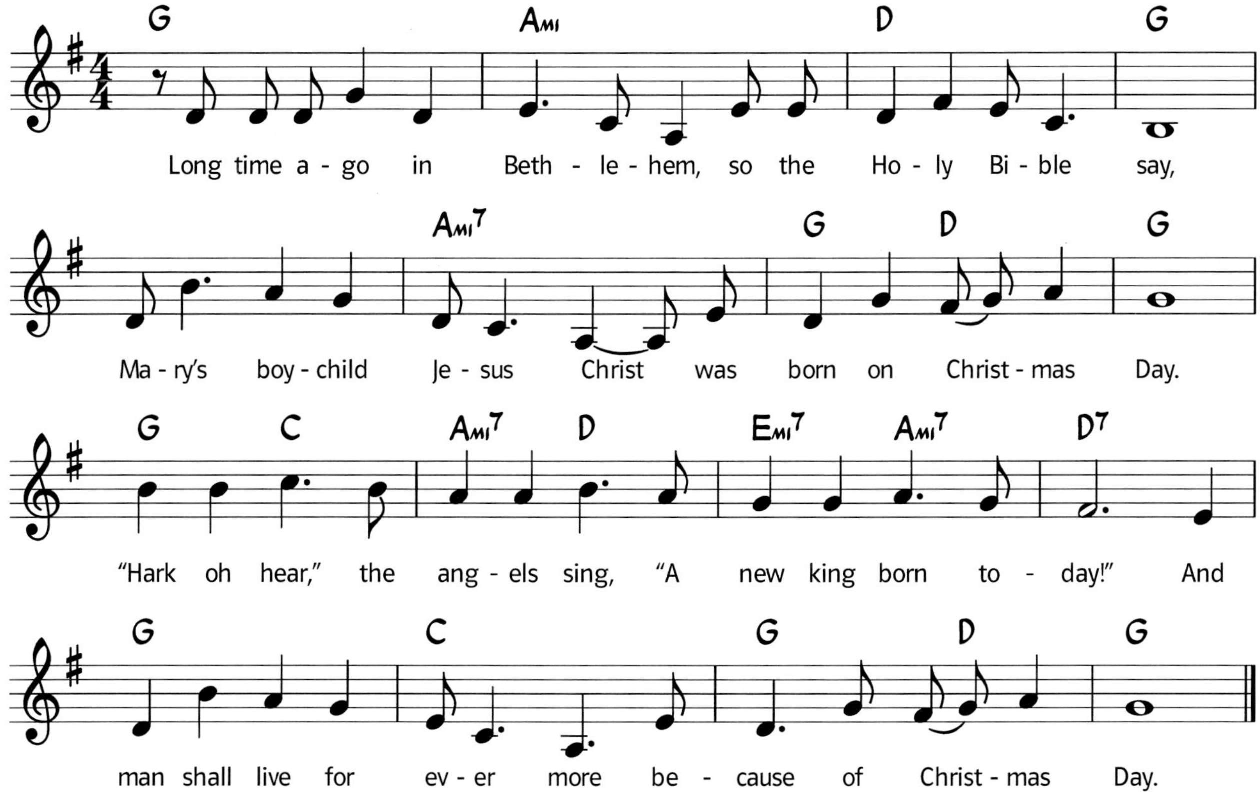

1. Long time ago in Bethlehem,
   So the Holy Bible say,
   Mary's boy-child Jesus Christ
   Was born on Christmas Day.

Chorus:

"Hark oh hear", the angels sing,
"A new king born today!"
And man shall live for ever more
Because of Christmas Day.

2. While shepherds watched their flocks by night
   They see a bright new shining star,
   Then the herald choir sing,
   The music seem to come from afar.

Chorus

3. Now Joseph and his wife Mary
   Came to Bethlehem that night,
   They find no place for to born the child;
   Not a single room was in sight.

Chorus

4. By-'n-by they find a little nook
   In a stable all forlorn,
   And in a manger cold and dark
   Mary's little boy-child was born.

Chorus

ISBN 978-3-12-512751-7

Klett

5 Happy New Year

Old One, lie down
Your journey is done.
Little New Year
Will rise with the sun.

(Eleanor Farjeon)

Happy New Year

24

The most traditional thing about New Year's Eve in England today is the singing of *Auld Lang Syne*. Some further information about New Year's Eve, which could be copied and given to more able students, is given below.
Auld Lang Syne should be sung by students standing in a circle. They should cross their arms in front of them and hold hands with their neighbours on either side. As they sing they should gently shake hands. This is how Auld Lang Syne is traditionally sung as the clocks strike twelve on New Year's Eve. The version on the CD is a modern arrangement of this traditional song.

New Year's Eve

There are no fireworks on New Year's Eve in Britain, but young people and adults often have lively parties on New Year's Eve.
In Scotland New Year's Eve is called "Hogmanay". Hogmanay is almost as important for the Scots as Christmas. Here, people go "first-footing": you visit friends and relatives as soon as the New Year has begun and try to be the first person through the front door. Traditionally a tall dark-haired person brought good luck to the house by bringing a piece of coal, some bread and some salt (for warmth, hospitality and health). Nowadays first-footers always take their own whisky with them! Children usually drink ginger wine or raspberry wine. People eat shortbread – a kind of biscuit –, black buns – dark fruit buns – and sultana cake. On the Channel Islands "Old Father Time" is buried in the sand to show that the end of an old year has come.
All over Britain it is common to make New Year's resolutions. These are promises you make to yourself and try to keep for the whole year.

New Year poems

25

The poem *Months of the year* provides the opportunity to practise the names of the months. The poem *The New Year* is a cheerful poem depicting the New Year as a person who has all sorts of gifts to offer. Ask students what they would like the New Year to bring them and/or what the last New Year brought them. Both poems can be learnt by heart by the students.

Make your own calendar

26

The items needed by students are listed on the worksheet.

Further activity

A class calendar

Divide the class into groups and ask each group to make one part of the calendar.

1. You will need twelve strips of card: one for each month. Each strip of card should be decorated with the name of the month, drawings and pictures.
2. You will need a long, narrow strip of card decorated and marked off from 1-31 for the days of the month.
3. You will need a date marker made from cardboard.
4. Put the months in the correct order. (You can make a game out of this by handing out the month cards to twelve students and then telling them they must line up in front of the class in the correct order as quickly as possible. You then call out the name of one month, and all the remaining students must line up behind this student. Give all the students behind the "month" a number [the first person is number 1 and so on]. Now call out the name of another month. All the students must line up behind this month. Number them again. Students must add the numbers they have been given together. Repeat this five times. The one with the lowest number at the end of the game is the winner.)
5. Punch two or three holes in the tops of the cards and string them together with ribbon or string.
6. Hang the date card down from the middle of the month, and fix the date marker over the correct date.

In addition to the calendar the students could also decorate 12 large sheets of paper, one for each month. They might write topical rhymes or poems on them. These posters can then be used to decorate the classroom throughout the year.

Make a Chinese lantern

27

Students follow the instructions on the worksheet. For decorating the lanterns they might use Chinese letters or numbers which can easily be found on the internet. The lanterns may be hung on strings to decorate the classroom around Chinese New Year.

The dates of the beginning of Chinese New Year from 2013 to 2020 are given in the grid in the information below.
This information can be given to the students (possibly in their mother tongue) before asking them to complete worksheets 27. and 28.

Chinese New Year

Chinese New Year is the most important festival for Chinese people all over the world. The Chinese follow a lunar calendar, so the date is different every year. The new year in the Chinese calendar begins on the second new moon after the winter solstice. It usually falls between the middle of January and the end of February.

The grid below gives the dates of the first day of Chinese New Year from 2013 to 2020.

Year	First day of Chinese New Year	Name of the year
2013	10th February	Snake
2014	31st January	Horse
2015	19th February	Sheep
2016	8th February	Monkey
2017	28th January	Rooster
2018	16th February	Dog
2019	5th February	Pig
2020	25th January	Rat

The celebrations of Chinese New Year last fifteen days.
On the days before the new year starts homes are thoroughly cleaned to make them ready for good luck and prosperity in the coming year. Houses, offices and factories are decorated with paper flowers, so-called flowers of prosperity.
On Chinese New Year's Eve there is a big family dinner (Reunion dinner). At midnight there are fireworks and everywhere you will hear the greeting "Kung hei fat choi" which means "Happy New Year". Groups of lion dancers dance from house to house to collect lucky money bags and vegetables which have been hung out for them. This is supposed to bring good luck.
Children also get lucky money bags, small red envelopes with money inside.

On the first days of Chinese New Year people visit relatives and friends, go to temples or other special events.
On the 15th day of Chinese New Year the Lantern Festival is celebrated. Lanterns of all sizes and shapes decorate houses and streets. There is music and dancing in the streets.

Many cities have parades with dragon or lion dancers.
"The San Francisco Chinese New Year Festival and Parade" is the oldest and largest celebration of Chinese New Year outside China.
Other big cities in English speaking countries which have large Chinese communities and therefore big parades to celebrate Chinese New Year are London, New York, Sydney, Toronto and Vancouver.

Chinese animal years

This worksheet offers a good opportunity to repeat or introduce names of animals and large numbers and dates. This should be done before students do the tasks on the worksheet.

28

Students may like to learn about the legend of the animals in the Chinese zodiac, and also about the characteristics assigned to people who were born in these particular years. This will probably be done in the students' mother tongue. Advanced students may be given the English texts.
It might also be an idea to write the names of the animals and the characteristics assigned to them on small cards. The cards are shuffled and students must find the matching pairs. This can be done in pairs or groups or even with the whole group via an overhead projector. Make sure that students are familiar with the vocabulary."

Each year in the Chinese calendar is named after an animal. There are several legends about how the animals were chosen for the Chinese calendar.
One legend goes that long ago the gods chose twelve animals the years should be named after. They arranged a swimming race across a river, and the first animal to get to the river bank would have the first year of the sequence of twelve years in the Chinese calendar.
When it came to the race the ox was about to win, but the clever rat which was a poor swimmer and had travelled on the ox's back, jumped off just before the ox approached the river bank and got there first. And so the first year in the Chinese zodiac became the Year of the Rat. The ox was second, so the second year is the Year of the Ox.
Next to arrive was the tiger, then the hare, the dragon, the snake, the horse, the ram, the monkey, the rooster and the dog, and last the pig.
Chinese people believe that people born in a particular year have characteristics similar to those of the animal which rules this year.

People born in the year of the ...	**are said to be ...**
RAT	ambitious, charming, cheerful, full of integrity, good at making friends, kind
OX	faithful, good at listening to others, patient, quiet,strong, stubborn
TIGER	brave, intelligent, powerful, respected by others
HARE	god-tempered, happy, lucky, successful
DRAGON	energetic, gentle, good rulers, healthy, honest
SNAKE	beautiful, careful, fortunate in money matters, wise
HORSE	cheerful, good with their hands, impulsive, popular, quick-witted, talented
RAM	artistic, compassionate, creative, fond of beautiful things, shy, sincere
MONKEY	clever, creative, good at making decisions, selfish, successful, vain, well-informed
ROOSTER	alert, inclined to express themselves in music or writing, outspoken, precise, proud, upright
DOG	conscientious, discreet, good friends, honest, loyal, straightforward
PIG	brave, courteous, good at making friendships for life, honest, shy, straightforward

Happy New Year

Auld Lang Syne

(words: Robert Burns music: traditional Scottish)

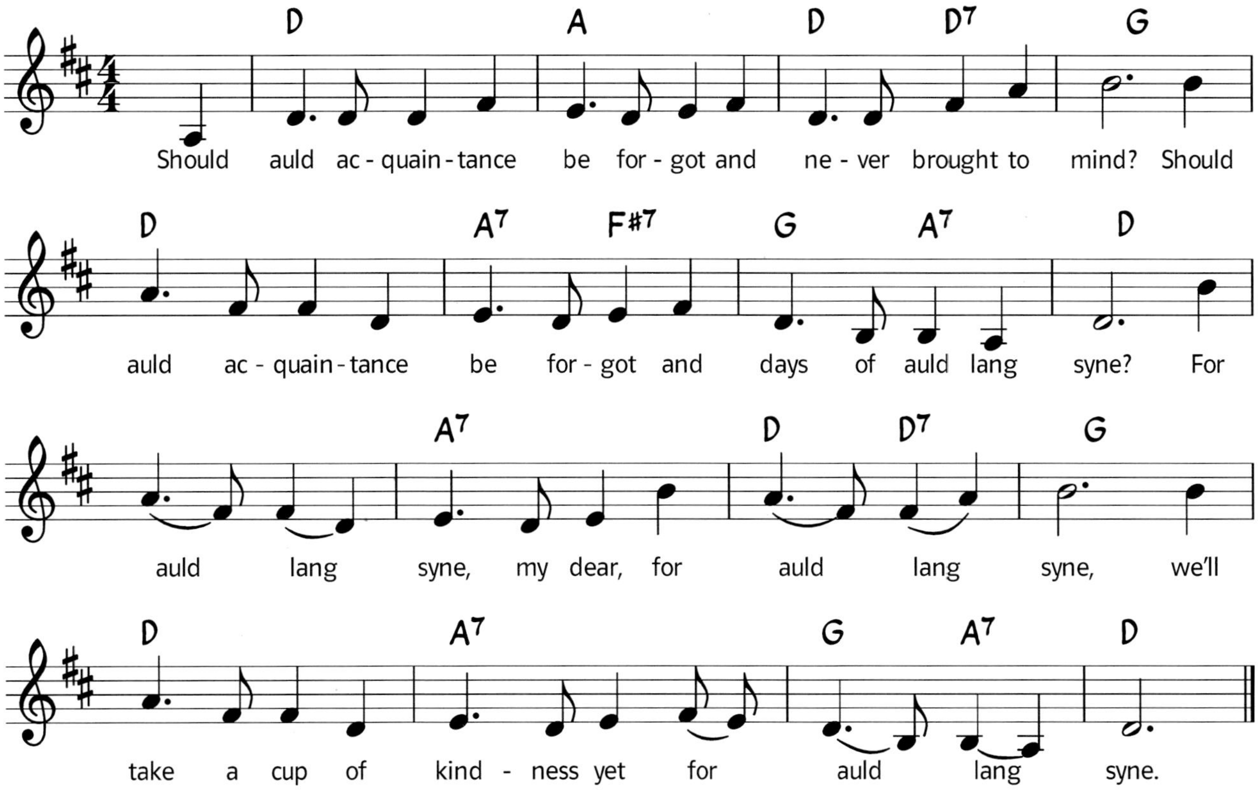

1. Should auld acquaintance be forgot
   And never brought to mind?
   Should auld acquaintance be forgot
   And days of auld lang syne?

   For auld lang syne, my dear,
   For auld lang syne,
   We'll take a cup of kindness yet
   For auld lang syne.

2. And there's a hand, my trusty friend,
   And give a hand of thine,
   We'll take a cup of kindness yet
   For auld lang syne.

   For auld lang syne, my dear,
   For auld lang syne,
   We'll take a cup of kindness yet
   For auld lang syne.

ISBN 978-3-12-512751-7

New Year poems

The New Year

I am the little New Year, ho, ho!
Here I come tripping in over the snow.
Shaking my bells with a merry din –
So open your doors and let me in!
Presents I bring for each and all –
Big folks, little folks, short and tall;
Each one from me a treasure may win –
So open your doors and let me in!
Some shall have silver and some shall have gold,
Some shall have new clothes and some shall have old;
Some shall have brass and some shall have tin –
So open your doors and let me in!
Some shall have water and some shall have milk
Some shall have satin and some shall have silk!
But each from me a present may win –
So open your doors and let me in!

(author unknown)

ISBN 978-3-12-512751-7

Make your own calendar

You will need a small box with a lid and some cardboard!

1. *Paint the box or cover it in nice paper.*

2. *Cut out thirteen strips of card the width of the box as follows:*
   a) *Cut two long strips 12 cms higher than the sides of the box. (Cards 1 and 2)*
   b) *Cut eight shorter strips 8 cms higher than the sides of the box. (Cards 3-10)*
   c) *Cut three even shorter strips 4 cms higher than the sides of the box. (Cards 11-13)*

3. *Draw a line 4 cms from the top and bottom on both sides of each card.*

4. *Cards 1 and 2 are for the days of the week. Write the days of the week on the cards in the spaces above the lines.*

5. *Cards 3-10 are for the days of the months. Write the numbers on them in the spaces above the lines.*

Card 1		Card 2	
FRONT	BACK	FRONT	BACK
Sunday	**Tuesday**	**Thursday**	**Saturday**
Monday	Wednesday	Friday	

Card 3		Card 4		Card 5		Card 6	
FRONT	BACK	FRONT	BACK	FRONT	BACK	FRONT	BACK
1	**3**	**5**	**7**	**9**	**11**	**13**	**15**
2	**4**	**6**	**8**	**10**	**12**	**14**	**16**

Card 7		Card 8		Card 9		Card 10	
FRONT	BACK	FRONT	BACK	FRONT	BACK	FRONT	BACK
17	**19**	**21**	**23**	**25**	**27**	**29**	**31**
18	**20**	**22**	**24**	**26**	**28**	**30**	

6. *Cards 11-13 are for the months of the year. Write the months on them in the spaces above the lines.*

Card 8		Card 9		Card 10	
FRONT	BACK	FRONT	BACK	FRONT	BACK
January	**March**	**May**	**July**	**September**	**November**
February	April	June	August	October	December

7. *Stand the lid of the box up at the back of the box and stick it to the box.*

8. *Now put the cards in the box in the right order.*

9. *Set the date by turning over the cards until you reach the right date for that day. When you come to the end of one card put it behind the other cards of the same size.*

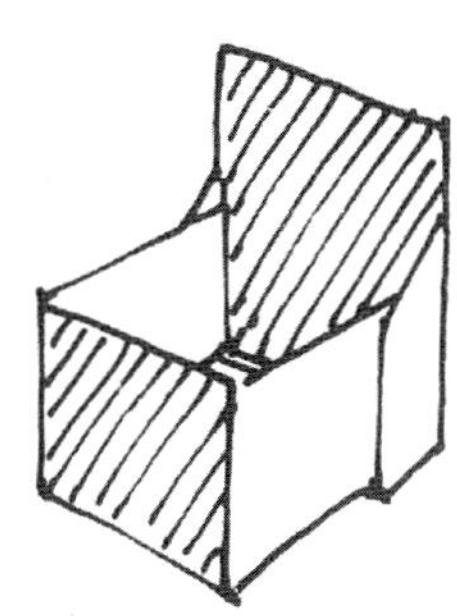

ISBN 978-3-12-512751-7

Make a Chinese lantern

You will need:

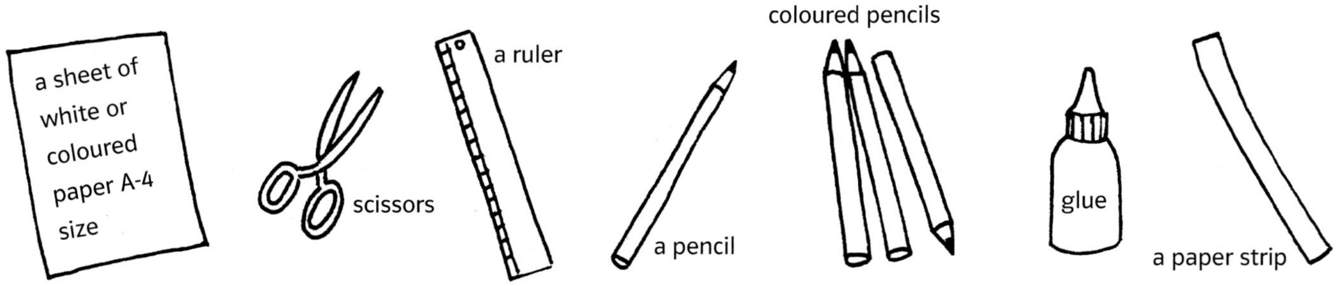

1. *Draw straight lines along the both long sides of the sheet of paper.*

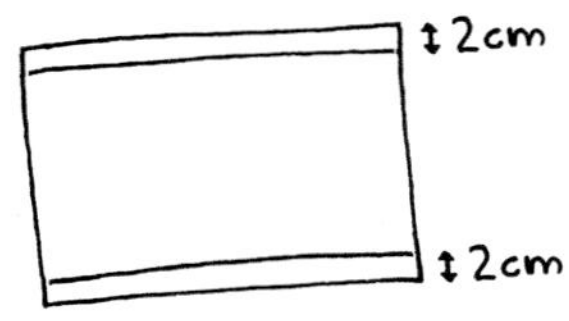

2. *Draw a pattern or a colourful picture between the lines.*

3. *Fold the sheet of paper in half.*

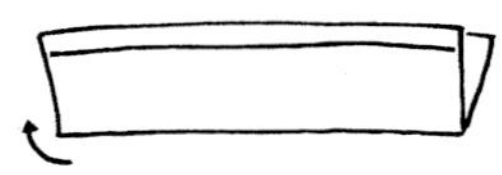

4. *Make straight cuts from the folded edge to the line.*

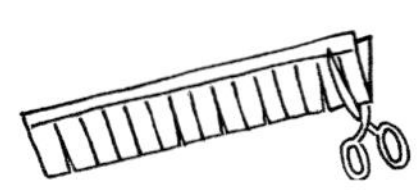

5. *Unfold the sheet and stick the two short sides together to form a lantern.*

6. *Glue the strip of paper on top of the lantern to form a handle.*

7. *You can hang your lantern on a piece of string to decorate the classroom.*

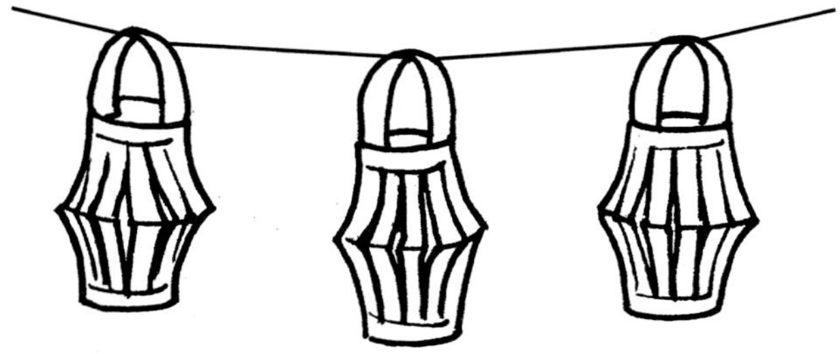

ISBN 978-3-12-512751-7

Chinese Animal Years

Chinese years are named after twelve animals. These are: the dog, the dragon, the hare, the horse, the monkey, the ox, the pig, the ram, the rat, the rooster, the snake and the tiger.

You can see pictures of these twelve animals and the years which are named after them.

1. *Write the names of the animals next to the pictures.*
2. *Find the year in which you (your father, mother, brother, sister, grandfather, grandmother, aunt, uncle, cousin, friend or ...) were born and tell your partner about.*

Example: **"I was born in two thousand and four. It was the year of the monkey."**
"My mother was born in nineteen seventy-six. It was ..."

____

1924, 1936, 1948, 1960,
1972, 1984, 1996, 2008

____

1925, 1937, 1949, 1961,
1973, 1985, 1997, 2009

____

1926, 1938, 1950, 1962,
1974, 1986, 1998, 2010

____

1927, 1939, 1951, 1963,
1975, 1987, 1999, 2011

____

1928, 1940, 1952, 1964,
1976, 1988, 2000, 2012

____

1929, 1941, 1953, 1965,
1977, 1989, 2001, 2013

____

1930, 1942, 1954, 1966,
1978, 1990, 2002, 2014

____

1931, 1943, 1955, 1967,
1979, 1991, 2003, 2015

____

1932, 1944, 1956, 1968,
1980, 1992, 2004, 2016

____

1933, 1945, 1957, 1969,
1981, 1993, 2005, 2017

____

1934, 1946, 1958, 1970,
1982, 1995, 2006, 2018

____

1935, 1947, 1959, 1971,
1983, 1995, 2007, 2019

ISBN 978-3-12-512751-7

6 In winter

All these activities are ideal for really wintry weather conditions. Of course they canbedone anytime during the winter, even if the weather outside is not "ideal"!

In Winter

29

In Winter can be sung or just listened to by students. Copy master 30 is a cloze text based on the song which can be used as a listening comprehension before the students are given the text to read.

The song could be sung as follows:
The teacher, a student or a group of students sings the complete song as it appears on the worksheet. The rest of the class sings only the words below printed in **bold** type (indicating that all students sing together) and in *italics* (indicating an echo: these parts overlap into the next line of the song and are only sung by those students not singing the complete song).

In winter, *(In winter)*
See the snowflakes falling by your window,
See the smiles of children when their cheeks glow,
When winter,
When winter is here.

In winter, *(In winter)*
Hear the crunch of footsteps on the hard snow,
Hear the keyholes whistle when the wind blows,
When winter,
When winter is here.

Sometimes ice and wind and sleet
Freeze your hands and wet your feet,
Make you want to stay indoors,
But I hate it when it thaws,
In winter, *(In winter)*

In winter, *(In winter)*
Feel the cold air biting on your red nose,
Feel the warmth of embers when a fire glows,
When winter,
When winter is here.

Sometimes ice and wind and sleet
Freeze your hands and wet your feet,
Make you want to stay indoors,
But I hate it when it thaws,
In winter, *(In winter)*
In winter, *(In winter)*
Yes, winter is here.

Game

Rhythmical call and response game

This game may be played to practise some of the vocabulary from the song, and can be played before or after doing the winter song. (It is also possible to play it independently of the song.) In this game the teacher introduces words from the song text (or other new words), and the students repeat them together three times. This is done in rhythm (see below) and the meaning of the words is shown clearly by pointing at the things, parts of the body, etc., as they are mentioned. The following words from *In Winter* can be used: nose, feet, smile, window, snow, hand, cheek.
Before starting the game practise the rhythm in which the words are to be called out. Count to four in a steady rhythm four times. Students can beat time with their feet. (It is important to keep time and not get faster during the game. A metronome might help you to stay in time.)
When everybody is familiar with the rhythm the game can begin. The teacher calls out some words from the song text in the rhythm described above. At the beginning it is advisable for the teacher to use the same word twice, e.g. nose – nose – feet – feet. The teacher points to the parts of the body as they are mentioned. The students repeat after the teacher three times in unison pointing to the parts of the body as they are mentioned. Then the teacher introduces another unit of words, e. g. nose – hand – window – smile. Again the students repeat after the teacher three times.

Variations:

a) Ask students to introduce their own units of four words.
b) Make units with less than four words but maintain the rhythm. (In this case one or more beats will be silent.)
c) Increase the number of words to be called out to eight but keep the same rhythm! For example: nose/nose – window/window – feet/feet – smile/smile.

In Winter: Listening comprehension

30

This is a cloze text based on the song *In Winter* (copy master 29) which can be used as a listening comprehension before students are given the text to read.
Introduce the song to the students via the CD (or by singing it yourself).
Ask the students for words and phrases they recognise. Ask them whether they like the song or not, and what kind of atmosphere the song describes.
Hand out the worksheet and ask students to listen to the song carefully and fill in the blanks on their worksheets. Play the song twice to allow enough time to work out the missing words.
You may want to put the missing words in the wrong order on the blackboard or overhead projector to help less able students.

Winter Poems

31

These poems are ideal to learn when it is snowing. Students can learn the poems by heart and illustrate their favourite one.
The first poem is an action poem. Divide the class into groups and ask each group to make up suitable actions to go with the verses. Students could draw pictures to go with the poem, which could be displayed in the classroom.

Solution to riddle:
A snowman.

Winter Word Search

32

The word search provides practice in some winter vocabulary. As an additional exercise students could be asked to work in groups and make up a winter story or short play in which all these words are used at least once. Then they can read their stories or act their plays to the class.

Solution

cold	ice-skating	snow
December	igloo	snowball
Eskimo	January	snowdrops
frost	sledging	snowflakes
frozen	sleigh	snowman
February	sleighing	white
ice	ski	winter

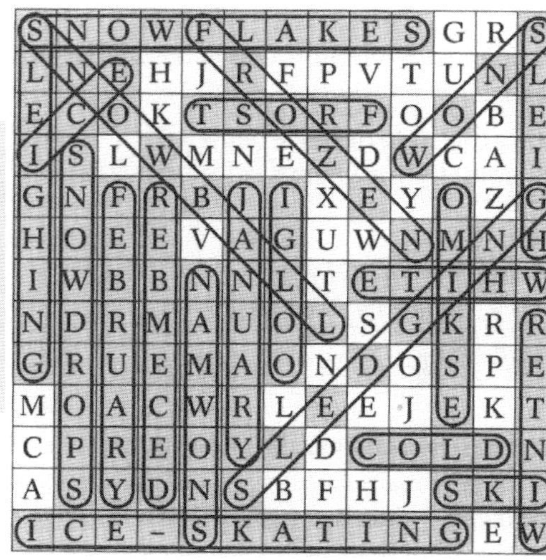

Draw a Winter Picture

16

Students will need pencils and coloured pencils (or equivalent).
This winter picture is a kind of comprehension exercise to show that students are familiar with winter vocabulary.
First have the students complete the heading of the picture, then give the students the following instructions. Before or while you read out the instructions, you may write the important vocabulary on the blackboard or overhead projector.

Draw a winter picture and colour it in. Draw
- children playing in the snow and a snowman on the right-hand side of the river;
- children with their sledges on the hill on the right;
- Father Christmas flying through the sky in his sleigh pulled by reindeer;
- a bunch of mistletoe on the wall of the house;
- a tree on the left-hand side of the house with its branches and twigs covered in snow;
- a Christmas tree on the right-hand side of the house; it is decorated with fairy lights, and it has a star on the top;
- snowflakes in the air.

In Winter

(words and music: Robert Metcalf)

In winter,
See the snowflakes falling by your window,
See the smiles of children when their cheeks glow.
When winter,
When winter is here.

In winter,
Hear the crunch of footsteps on the hard snow,
Hear the keyholes whistle when the wind blows,
When winter,
When winter is here.

Sometimes ice and wind and sleet
Freeze your hands and wet your feet,
Make you want to stay indoors,
But I hate it when it thaws,
In winter.

In winter,
Feel the cold air biting on your red nose,
Feel the warmth of embers when a fire glows,
When winter,
When winter is here.

Sometimes ice and wind and sleet
Freeze your hands and wet your feet,
Make you want to stay indoors,
But I hate it when it thaws,
In winter,
In winter,
Yes, winter is here.

ISBN 978-3-12-512751-7

In Winter: Listening comprehension

Listen to the song and fill in the missing words.

In winter,
See the ________________ falling by your ________________,
See the smiles of. ________________. when their cheeks glow,
When ________________,
When winter is ________________.

In winter,
the crunch of footsteps on the hard ________________,
Hear the keyholes whistle when the ________________ blows.
When ________________,
When winter is ________________.

Sometimes ________________ and ________________ and sleet
Freeze your ________________ and wet your ________________.
Make you want to ________________ indoors,
But I hate it when it thaws,
In winter.

In winter,
Feel the ________________ air biting on your red ________________,
Feel the warmth of embers when a ________________ glows,
When ________________,
When winter is ________________.

Sometimes ________________ and ________________ and sleet
Freeze your ________________ and wet your ________________.
Make you want to ________________ indoors,
But I hate it when it thaws,
In winter, In winter, Yes, winter is here.

ISBN 978-3-12-512751-7

Winter Poems 31

Snowflakes

This is how snowflakes play about,
Up in cloudland they dance in and out.

This is how they whirl down the street,
Powdering everybody they meet.

This is how they come fluttering down,
Whitening the roads, the fields, and the town.

This is how snowflakes cover the trees,
Each branch and twig bends in the breeze.

This is how snowflakes blow in a heap,
Looking just like fleecy sheep.

This is how they cover the ground,
Cover it thickly with never a sound.

This is how people shiver and shake
On a snowy morning when first they wake.

This is how snowflakes melt away,
When the sun sends out its beams to play.

Cold and raw the north winds blow
Bleak in the morning early;
All the hills are covered with snow.
And winter's now come fairly.

Snowdrops

I like to think
That, long ago,
There fell to earth
Some flakes of snow
Which loved this cold,
Grey world of ours
So much, they stayed
As snowdrop flowers.

(Mary Vivian)

A winter riddle

What is it?
Roll him and roll him until he is big.
Roll him until he is fat as a pig.
He has two eyes and a hat on his head.
He'll stand there all night,
While we go to bed.

ISBN 978-3-12-512751-7

Winter Word Search

Here are some "wintry" words.

frost	snowflakes	sledging
frozen	snowman	sleigh
February	white	sleighing
ice	winter	ski
ice-skating	cold	snow
igloo	December	snowball
January	Eskimo	snowdrops

Can you find them in the word square?

↓↑ ⇄ ↗↙ ↘↖

The first one is done for you.

S	N	O	W	F	L	A	K	E	S	G	R	S
L	N	E	H	J	R	F	P	V	T	U	N	L
E	C	O	K	T	S	O	R	F	O	O	B	E
I	S	L	W	M	N	E	Z	D	W	C	A	I
G	N	F	R	B	J	I	X	E	Y	O	Z	G
H	O	E	E	V	A	G	U	W	N	M	N	H
I	W	B	B	N	N	L	T	E	T	I	H	W
N	D	R	M	A	U	O	L	S	G	K	R	R
G	R	U	E	M	A	O	N	D	O	S	P	E
M	O	A	C	W	R	L	E	E	J	E	K	T
C	P	R	E	O	Y	L	D	C	O	L	D	N
A	S	Y	D	N	S	B	F	H	J	S	K	I
I	C	E	–	S	K	A	T	I	N	G	G	W

ISBN 978-3-12-512751-7

7 Be my Valentine

The activities in this section should all be done on and around Valentine's Day, 14th February.

Valentine Songs

33

These three songs are sung in B^b major on the CD, not in C major as in the music on the copy master. They are sung as a medley with short spoken links between each song.

A Valentine Round

The tune this round is set to (Kookaburra) is probably already known by many students. First sing the song altogether. Then divide the class into two groups and sing it in two parts. The second group can come in after two or four bars (at the end of the first or second line of the verse). Then the class can be divided into four groups, each group comes in every two bars (when the first line of the verse has been sung by the previous group).

I sent a letter to my love

This song is the accompaniment to a popular children's game. You will need a handkerchief (or cloth). It is played by British children throughout the year and not just on Valentine's Day.

1. The students stand in a circle.
2. While they sing the song one student (A) walks clockwise around the outside of the circle carrying the handkerchief in one hand.
3. On "dropped it" the student drops the handkerchief behind one of the students (B) in the circle.
4. Whilst the last two lines of the song are sung, students A and B run around the circle: A clockwise, B anticlockwise. Both try to reach the empty place in the circle.
5. The student who fails to reach the space becomes the next one to walk around the circle with the handkerchief, whilst the song is sung again.

Pretty little Dutch girl

This is a traditional clapping rhyme. It can be played at other times, too.
Students sit or stand in twos facing each other. They repeat the following clapping sequence whilst singing the song:

Version 1

Text	Actions
I	–
am	Clap hands on knees.
a	–
pretty	Clap own hands.
little	–
Dutch girl	Clap against partner's hands.
–	Clap own hands.
as	–
pretty	Clap hands on knees.
as	–
I	Clap own hands.
can	–
be	Clap against partner's hands.
–	Clap own hands.
(etc.)	(etc.)

Version 2

In this version the clapping is done twice as quickly.

Text	Actions
I	–
am	Clap hands on knees.
a	Clap own hands.
pretty	Right hand claps against partner's right hand.
little	Clap own hands.
Dutch	Left hand claps against partner's left hand.
girl	Clap own hands.
–	Clap against both of partner's hands.
as	Clap own hands.
(pretty, etc.)	(Clap hands on knees, etc.)

Repeat the song becoming faster each time.
You could also suggest that the boys sing "I am a handsome little Dutch boy" and substitute girl for boy, her for his, etc., throughout the song.

34

Valentine's Day

This worksheet gives some information about Valentine's Day and some instructions for sending messages in secret codes.

35

Make your own Valentine's card

Students will need paper, coloured pencils (or equivalent) and glue. Students can make their own Valentine cards using this worksheet.

Valentine Songs

A Valentine Round

(words: trad./B. Schanz-Hering; music: trad.)

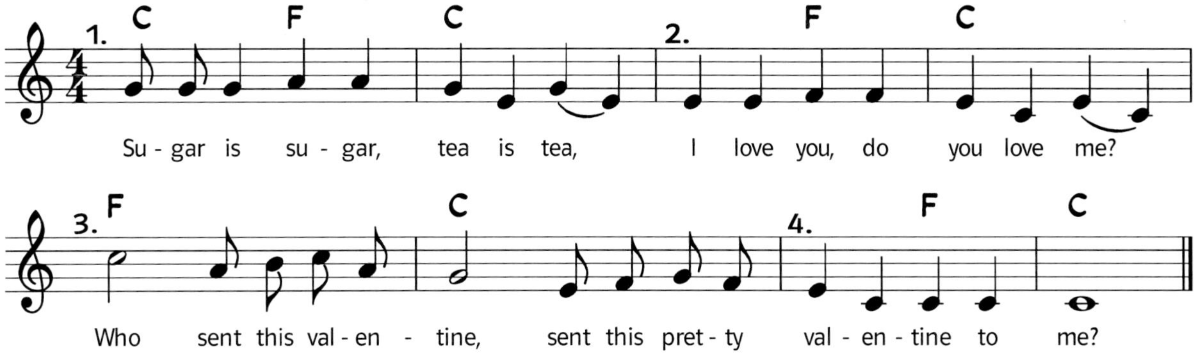

Sugar is sugar, tea is tea,
I love you, do you love me?

Who sent this valentine,
Sent this pretty valentine to me?

I sent a letter to my love

(words and music: traditional)

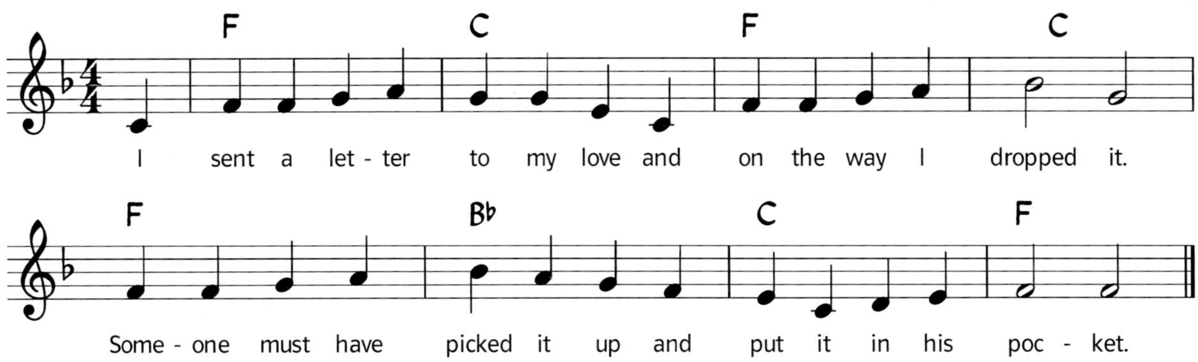

I sent a letter to my love
And on the way I dropped it,

Someone must have picked it up
And put it in his pocket.

Pretty little Dutch girl

(words and music: traditional)

I am a pretty little Dutch girl,
As pretty as I can be.
And all the boys in the neighbourhood
Are crazy over me.

My boyfriend's name is Mellow,
He comes from the land of Jello,
With pickles for his toes
And a cherry for his nose
And that's the way my story goes.

ISBN 978-3-12-512751-7

Valentine's Day

February 14th is called Valentine's Day in Britain. On Valentine's Day you can send cards to people you love or like a lot. But you don't put your name in the cards: the person has to guess who the card is from! People in Britain also send flowers and small presents to each other on Valentine's Day. The person you send your card to is called your "Valentine"! Most people send Valentine cards just for fun!

Most cards have a poem in them. Here are some examples:

Sending a secret message

You could send a Valentine message using a secret code. Here is a simple one:
Write the letters of the alphabet on one line, and then write them backwards on the next line.
Now use the letters in the second line, not the normal letters. So, for example, DOG becomes WLT.

A	B	C	D	E	F	G	H	I	J	K	L	M	N	O	P	Q	R	S	T	U	V	W	X	Y	Z
Z	Y	X	W	V	U	T	S	R	Q	P	O	N	M	L	K	J	I	H	G	F	E	D	C	B	A

You can also make codes using numbers, for example:

A	B	C	D	E	F	G	H	I	J	K	L	M	N	O	P	Q	R	S	T	U	V	W	X	Y	Z
6	7	8	9	10	11	12	13	14	15	16	17	18	19	20	21	22	23	24	25	26	1	2	3	4	5

9/20 4/20/26 17/14/16/10 24/10/8/23/10/25 8/20/9/10/24 ? Yes!!

ISBN 978-3-12-512751-7

Make your own Valentine's card

1. *Decorate the two hearts on this page:*
   - Join the dots on the first heart to make a message.
   - Write a poem or a message (in a secret code perhaps) on the other heart
   - Write: To ___________ (your Valentine's name).
   - Don't write your name.
2. *Cut both hearts out.*
3. *Stick the hearts together.*
4. *Send/give your "card" to your Valentine.*

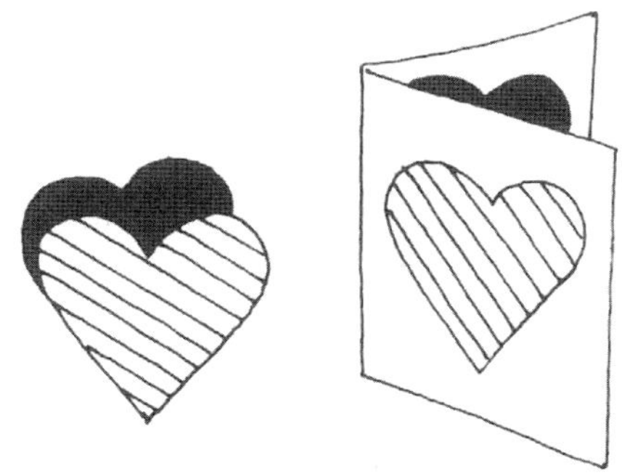

Instead of sticking the hearts together you could fold a piece of card in half and then stick the first heart on the front and the second on the inside.

ISBN 978-3-12-512751-7

8 Pancake Day

These activities are intended for use around Shrove Tuesday/Ash Wednesday in February. Whilst this period is known as Carnival time in many parts of Europe it should be pointed out to students that in fact "Carnival" is not celebrated in Britain. (Fancy dress parties traditionally take place at New Year and Halloween, and Christmas is the time when British people decorate their houses with paper chains and balloons, etc.) There are, however, carnivals throughout the year in Britain: most towns have a carnival with processions, entertainment, etc. The most famous carnival in Britain is the Notting Hill Carnival, which takes place in London's Notting Hill each summer on the last Monday in August (August Bank Holiday). It is a traditional West Indian festival, which was started by the many immigrants who have come to London from the West Indies.

Shrove Tuesday

36 This is a traditional English song. When students sing the song they should be given information about Pancake Day in Britain. (See below.)

Pancake Day

37 The ingredients for making pancakes are given on the worksheet. Some additional information about Pancake Day, which could be copied and given to more able students, is given below. This could be presented to students in their mother tongue. Perhaps you can organise a pancake race for students and/or staff.

Pancake Day

Pancake Day is another name for Shrove Tuesday. At one time people were not allowed to eat milk, eggs or fat during Lent, so they made pancakes to use up all these things. Nowadays, of course, you can eat what you like during Lent, but people still traditionally eat pancakes on Pancake Day – and often at no other time of the year! In Britain pancakes are usually eaten with sugar and lemon juice!
On Pancake Day there are often pancake races. People line up in the street holding a frying pan with a pancake in it. Somebody signals the start: "Ready, steady, go!" On "go" the racers run along the street "tossing their pancakes", that is, throwing them up into the air to turn them and catching them again in the frying pans. The first person to reach the finishing line or the end of the street is the winner!

Colour the clown

38 Students will need coloured pencils (or equivalent).
This worksheet enables students to learn or practise the words for parts of the body, clothes and colours. It can be used equally well at other times of the year. Instructions for students are given on the worksheet. Students could also be asked to draw their favourite fancy dress costume and describe it to the class, to a group or to a partner. This could also be done as a written exercise.

Carnival Nights

39

This song has been written especially for use when Carnival is being celebrated and especially in places where students come to school in fancy dress.
First play the CD or sing the song so that students are familiar with the words and the music.
Ask everybody to sing the first verse and dance along to it. During the other verses, only those who are dressed up as the characters in the verse sing and dance. The others stand still. (Alternatively, everyone can sing, but only the characters dance.) At the end all the students sing and dance together again.
Additional or alternative verses can easily be made according to the fancy dress worn by the students.

Game

Play *Vampires* (again). See page 24 for instructions on how to play.

Notting Hill Carnival

40

The worksheet and the information about Notting Hill Carnival can be given to the students either around carnival time (which is usually in February or early March) or in late August when Notting Hill Carnival is celebrated in London.

Notting Hill Carnival

Every year on the last weekend in August (August bank holiday) the streets of West London come alive with sounds of steel bands, smells of exotic food and sights of fantastic costumes. It is Notting Hill Carnival, a celebration of multicultural British life which takes place on the streets of London's Notting Hill.

Notting Hill Carnival was started in 1964 as a local festival by immigrants from the Caribbean island Trinidad and has taken place every year since then. It has become London's biggest street festival and has attracted around one million people in the last years – among them many tourists from all over the world.

The first day of the carnival, Sunday, is Children's Day, a day with special events for families and their children. There is a children's parade, lots of play areas and many activities for children and young people.

The main attraction of the Notting Hill Carnival is the parade for adults on Carnival Monday. It consists of twenty miles of astonishing floats playing Caribbean, African or South American music. You will see colourful costumes, often beautifully decorated with multi-coloured feathers. It can take up to a year to prepare the floats and costumes for the parade. It is not only the performers in the parade who wear costumes, but also many spectators dress up for the event.

The parade usually starts around 9 a.m. and finishes around 7 p.m. There are more than forty sound stages that line its route where people can listen to music and dance. The traditional sound of the festival is the music of the steel band, a group of musicians who play on drums that are made of empty oil containers. Other kinds of music that are characteristic for Notting Hill Carnival are calypso – typical Caribbean carnival music – , reggae, jazz, rap and hip-hop.

A visit to Notting Hill Carnival would be incomplete without trying some of the tasty food from the hundreds of food stalls lining the streets. They are selling all kinds of food and drink, especially Caribbean food, such as jerk chicken, goat curry, corn on the cob, rice and peas, fried bananas (plantain) and coconut juice.

Shrove Tuesday

(words and music: traditional English)

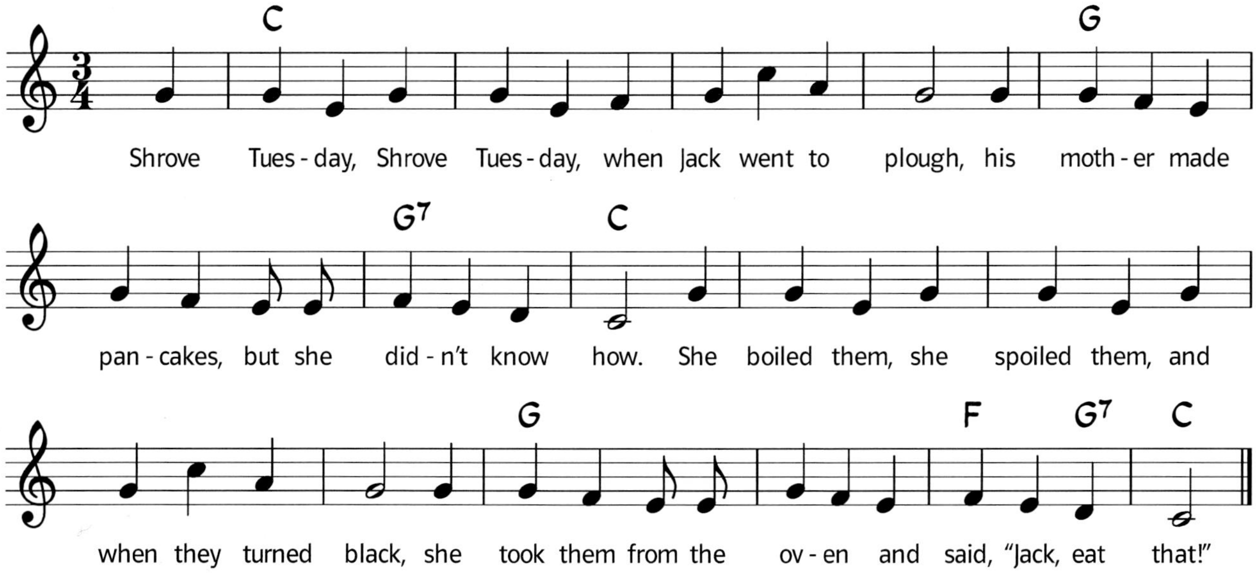

1. Shrove Tuesday, Shrove Tuesday,
   When Jack went to plough,
   His mother made pancakes,
   But she didn't know how.
   She boiled them, she spoiled them,
   And when they turned black,
   She took them from the oven
   And said, "Jack, eat that!"

2. Jack's mother made a pudding,
   'Twas done in an hour.
   She hadn't no eggs
   And she hadn't no flour
   She hadn't no figs
   And she hadn't no fat.
   She dapped it on the table
   And said, "Jack, eat that!"

3. Shrove Tuesday, Ash Wednesday,
   Jack's father's to plough.
   His mother made pancakes,
   But she didn't know how.
   She turned them, she burned them,
   And made them so black,
   She put too much pepper
   And poisoned poor Jack.

ISBN 978-3-12-512751-7

Pancake Day

The pancake

Mix a pancake,
Stir a pancake,
Pop it in the pan.

Fry the pancake,
Toss the pancake,
Catch it if you can.
(Christina Rossetti)

A Recipe: Pancakes

(Makes 10 thin pancakes.)

You will need:

100 g flour
a pinch of salt
1 egg
125 ml milk, 125 ml water, mixed
a tablespoon of cooking oil
cooking oil for frying
sugar, lemon juice, (jam)

1. Sift the flour and salt into a bowl.
2. Add the egg and half of the milk-water mixture.
3. Beat to a smooth batter.
4. Stir in the rest of the milk and water and the tablespoon of cooking oil.
5. Heat enough cooking oil to cover the bottom of a frying pan.
6. Pour in enough batter to coat the pan thinly.
7. Fry the pancake on one side, then turn over and fry on the other side.
8. Put the pancakes on a plate and serve with sugar and lemon juice (or jam).

ISBN 978-3-12-512751-7

Colour the clown

Colour the clown, please. Write down which colours you have used.

	Colour used
arms	
braces	
buttons	
bow-tie	
eyes	
face	
gloves	
hat	
hair	
legs	
mouth	
nose	
shirt	
socks	
trousers	
left shoe	
right shoe	
heels of shoes	
soles of shoes	

ISBN 978-3-12-512751-7

Carnival Nights

(words: trad./Wolfgang E. Hering/Brigitte Schanz-Hering; music: traditional)

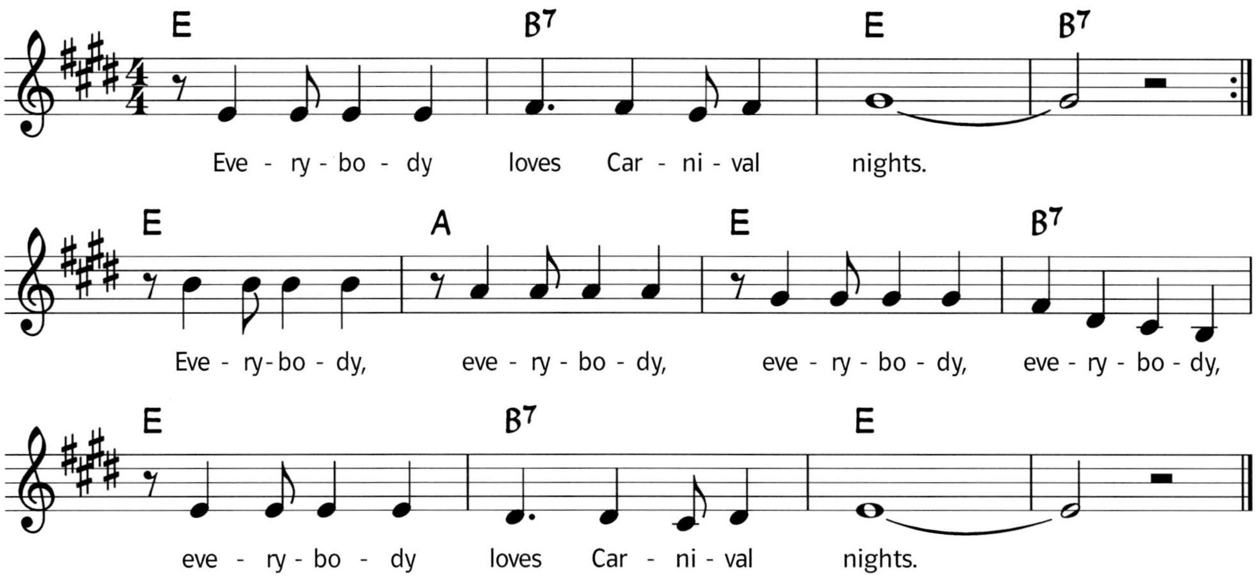

1. Everybody loves Carnival nights,
   Everybody loves Carnival nights,
   Everybody, everybody, everybody, everybody,
   Everybody loves Carnival nights.

2. All the cowboys love Carnival nights,
   All the cowboys love Carnival nights,
   All the cowboys, all the cowboys,
   all the cowboys, all the cowboys,
   All the cowboys love Carnival nights.

3. All the Indians love Carnival nights, ...

4. Kings and queens love ....

5. All the clowns love ....

6. Cats and mice love ....

7. All the others love ....

8. Everybody loves ....

ISBN 978-3-12-512751-7

Notting Hill Carnival

The most famous carnival in Britain is the Notting Hill Carnival. It takes place in Notting Hill in the West of London on the last Sunday and Monday in August (August bank holiday).
It is a Caribbean street carnival, very much like the famous Carnival in Rio, with steel bands, big parades, beautiful costumes and tasty Caribbean food. In the last years more than one million people from all over the world have come to Notting Hill to enjoy the event.

A Caribbean recipe – Fried banana (plantain)

You will need:

four ripe bananas
cooking oil
icing sugar

1. *Peel the bananas and cut them into 1cm-thick diagonal slices.*
2. *Heat cooking oil in a frying pan.*
3. *Put the banana slices into the hot oil and cook for two or three minutes until they get golden brown.*
4. *Take the fried banana slices out from the oil and put them on paper towels to drain.*
5. *Dust with icing sugar.*

They are great for dessert topped with vanilla ice cream.

Make a carnival mask

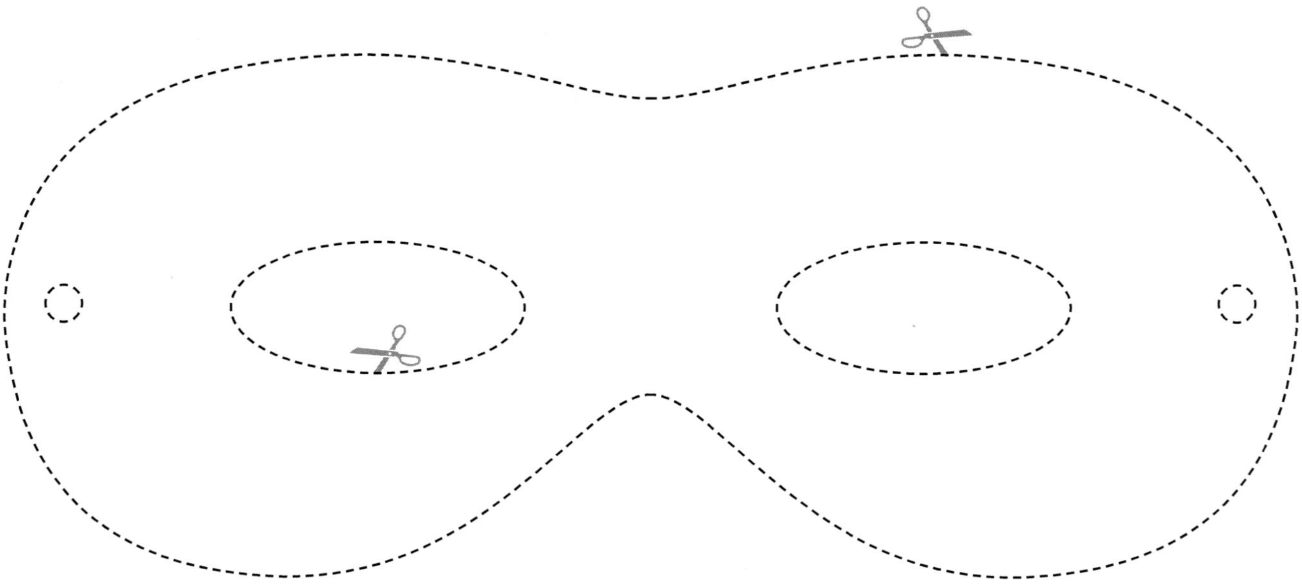

1. *Copy the mask pattern onto construction paper.*
2. *Cut out the holes for the eyes and punch holes at both sides.*
3. *Colour the mask with paints or crayons and decorate with glitter, feathers, fabric, buttons, beads and more.*
4. *Wear your mask at carnival or have an exhibition in the classroom.*

ISBN 978-3-12-512751-7

9 Spring is coming

The activities and worksheets in this chapter cover Mother's Day and April Fools' Day as well as being concerned generally with spring.

Spring is coming

41

This fairly simple song expresses the typical things associated with the beginning of spring. After listening to and singing the song, ask students to draw pictures to illustrate the song as a whole, or the individual verses. Use the pictures to decorate your classroom.

There are also two spring poems on the copy master. *The Caterpillar* is an action poem. When students are familiar with the text, ask them to make up actions to go with it. Alternatively they can make the following actions:

Text	Movements
A caterpillar crawled to the top of a tree. "I think I'll take a nap," said he.	Fingers of right hand "crawl" from the left shoulder to the left hand.
So – under a leaf he began to creep	Fingers of right hand "creep" under left hand.
To spin a cocoon;	Left hand encloses right hand.
Then he fell asleep.	Fold both hands; lay head on them.
All winter he slept in his cocoon bed.	Raise both hands; left hand encloses right hand.
Till Spring came along one day and said, "Wake up, wake up, little sleepyhead. Wake up, it's time to get out of bed."	Left hand grips right wrist and shakes it.
So – he opened his eyes that sunshiny day.	Open fingers of right hand.
Lo! He was a butterfly – and flew away.	Pretend to be flying.

O Dandelion: Students can draw pictures to go with the poem. They could draw the different stages of a dandelion, for example.

Spring Picture Crossword

42

This crossword practises some vocabulary for the birds and flowers which are typical of spring

Solution

Across	Down
4. violet	1. bird
6. nest	2. dandelion
8. caterpillar	3. butterfly
9. daffodil	5. tulip
	7. bee
	8. cat

Tulips and Daffodils

43

This is just for fun! Students will need coloured pencils (or equivalent). When they have finished they could be asked to describe their pictures to one another in short dialogues. For example:
A: "I've got three yellow tulips. How many yellow tulips have you got?"
B: "I've only got two. My vase is blue and red. What colour is your vase?"

Make your own Mother's Day card

44

Students will need scissors, glue, coloured pencils (or equivalent), stiff paper/thin card. Either make this card before Easter for the British Mother's Day (see below), or prior to Mother's Day in the students' own country. The additional information below could be copied and given to more able students.

Mother's Day

Mother's Day in Britain is always the fourth Sunday in Lent. It has been celebrated in Britain for more than three centuries. At one time it was usual for apprentices and servants working away from their families to be given a holiday on this day, so that they could visit their mothers. They often took their mothers a cake and perhaps some flowers. Flowers and chocolates are still traditional Mother's Day presents today. And, of course, there are Mother's Day cards, which are sold in huge quantities. Mother's Day in Britain today is really as much a commercial as a traditional event. (In the USA Mother's Day is celebrated on the 2nd Sunday in May each year.)

April Fool

45

This song describes the typical mood of April Fools' Day, especially for children. Use the information given below and tell students a little about April Fools' Day (1st April) in Britain before singing the song with them. The information could be copied and given to more able students. It could be given to less able students in their mother tongue. Ask students to describe any good tricks which they could play on April Fools' Day. Students could draw pictures to go with the song.

April Fools' Day

April 1st is known as April Fools' Day or All Fools' Day. On April 1st people play tricks on each other – but only between midnight and midday. Typical tricks are things like telling someone that their shoelaces are undone (when they're not, of course!) and putting an upturned empty eggshell in someone's eggcup at the breakfast table. You might find salt in the sugar bowl or someone else's schoolbooks in your bag. When you trick someone successfully you call them: "April Fool!" Even in the newspapers and on the radio and television news there are April Fools' jokes. They are often so well disguised that thousands of people believe them and are made "April Fools" by the media! Of course, students often play April Fools' tricks on their teachers, like hiding the chalk, putting drawing pins on the teacher's chair and swopping classrooms with another class!

Spring is coming

(words and music: trad.)

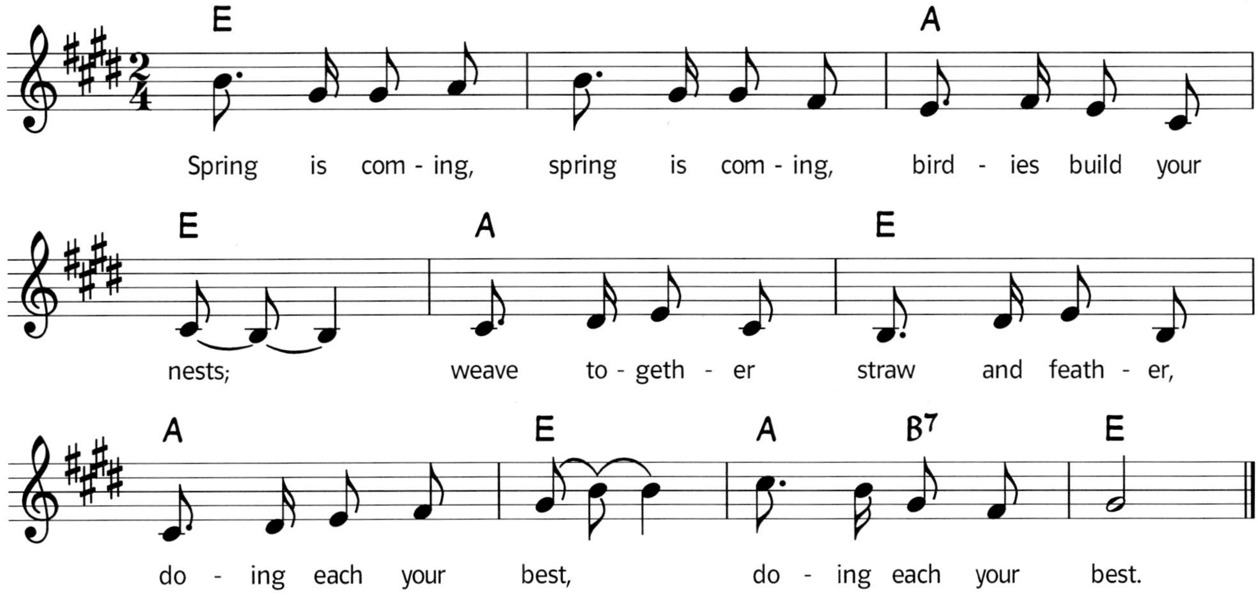

1. Spring is coming, spring is coming,
   Birdies build your nests;
   Weave together straw and feather,
   Doing each your best, doing each your best.

2. Spring is coming, spring is coming,
   Flowers are coming too,
   Pansies, lilies, daffodilies,
   Spring is nearly through, spring is nearly through.

3. Spring is coming, spring is coming,
   All around is fair,
   Shiver, quiver on the river,
   Spring is ev'rywhere, spring is ev'rywhere.

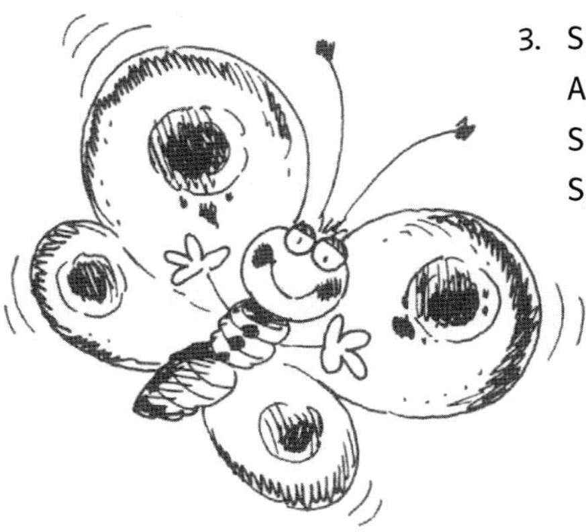

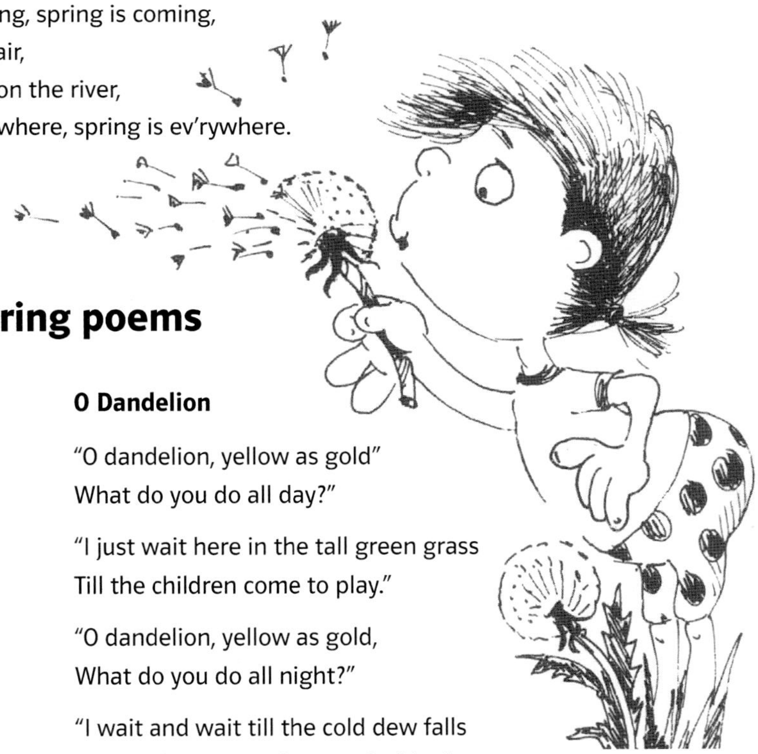

Two spring poems

The caterpillar

A caterpillar crawled to the top of a tree,
"I think I'll take a nap," said he.
So – under a leaf he began to creep
To spin a cocoon;
Then he fell asleep
All winter he slept in his cocoon bed,
Till Spring came along one day and said,
"Wake up, wake up, little sleepyhead.
Wake up, it's time to get out of bed."
So – he opened his eyes that sunshiny day.
Lo! He was a butterfly – and flew away!

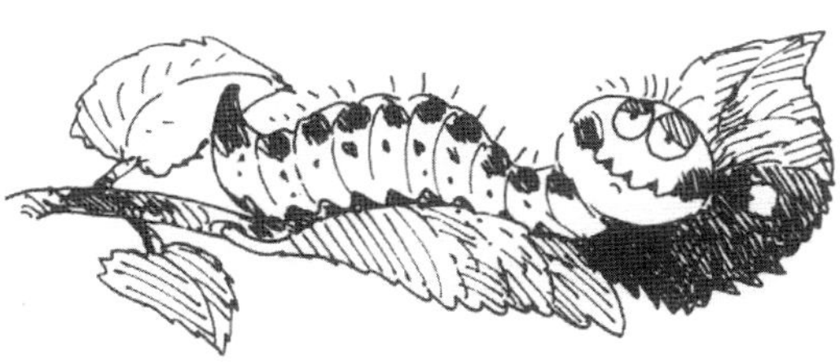

O Dandelion

"O dandelion, yellow as gold"
What do you do all day?"

"I just wait here in the tall green grass
Till the children come to play."

"O dandelion, yellow as gold,
What do you do all night?"

"I wait and wait till the cold dew falls
And my hair grows long and white."

"And what do you do when your hair is white
And the children come to play?"

"They take me up in their dimpled hands
And blow my hair away."

ISBN 978-3-12-512751-7

Spring Picture Crossword

Can you find the words in the letters below? Colour them in.

ISBN 978-3-12-512751-7

Klett

Tulips and Daffodils

1. Find your way through the flowers.

2. Colour the picture in.

ISBN 978-3-12-512751-7

Make your own Mother's Day card

Make this card and give it to your Mum on Mother's Day.

1. *Cut out the pictures of presents around the outside of the square.*
2. *Stick the presents in the right places on the table*
3. *Colour the picture in.*
4. *Cut the picture out.*
5. *Take a piece of card twice the size of the picture and fold it in half.*
6. *Stick your picture on it.*
7. *Inside your card write:*

Perhaps you can make a Father's Day card, too. In England Father's Day is the third Sunday in June.

ISBN 978-3-12-512751-7

April Fool

(author unknown)

1. Your hair is the colour of tomato soup,
   April Fool, April Fool!
   There's a great big gorilla in the chicken coop,
   April April Fool

Chorus:

Oh look out of the window, what do you see?
Peaches on the cherry tree.
I fool you, you fool me.
This is April Fools's Day.

2. The Cat's in the middle of the custard pie,
   April Fool, April Fool!
   There's a dog in the kitchen and he's ten feet high,
   April April Fool

   Chorus

3. The pig in the parlour has a big cigar,
   April Fool, April Fool!
   There's a two headed elephant in daddy's car,
   April April Fool.

   Chorus

4. The cow in the clover gave the horse a kiss,
   April Fool, April Fool!
   You can't ever sing a silly song like this
   Except on April Fools' Day.
   Only April first.

ISBN 978-3-12-512751-7

10 Easter Time

These copy masters are intended for use before the Easter holidays.

Easter in Britain

46

Give the students the background information below about Easter in Britain before giving them the worksheet. The information could be given in the mother tongue or copied and handed out to more able students. The words in the text printed in bold type appear in the exercise on copy master 46. On this worksheet there is a simple song to the tune of the American song "Down by the station". It can be sung as a round, with a rhythmical accompaniment, or as an action song.

Easter in Britain

When British children think of Easter they often think of one thing in particular: chocolate! On Easter Sunday people give each other **Easter eggs**. These are large eggs made of chocolate, which usually have smaller chocolates inside them. They are usually exchanged at the breakfast table.
On Easter Sunday people often eat hard-boiled eggs for breakfast. Some people colour these eggs or draw faces on them, though this is not a widespread tradition. **Easter bunnies**, daffodils and lambs are all closely associated with Easter and are often featured on Easter cards. At Easter people wish each other a **"Happy Easter"**. The Friday before Easter is called Good Friday. It is a public holiday, as is Easter Monday, the Monday after Easter. On Good Friday people traditionally eat **Hot cross buns** (see recipe, copy master 48) for breakfast. Today not many people make their own buns, they buy them! There are one or two games which started as Easter games, but are now played at any time of year at parties. For example: **egg-shackling**, **egg-rolling** and **egg-and-spoon races**.

The Easter Bunnies

A round: First practise the clapping which occurs in the last line of the song. Then, when the students are familiar with the words and the tune, divide the class into four groups. Each group comes in when the first line of the song has been sung by the previous group (every four bars). Give the students a signal telling them when they should stop singing if you want them to finish all together. Alternatively, tell each group to sing the song twice and then stop.

Rhythmical accompaniment: Clap hands alternately on legs and then hands together for the first three lines of the song. On "Ready, steady" stamp first the right and then the left foot on each syllable. Clap three times to the rhythm of "clap, clap, clap". Make no accompaniment to "off they go".

Action song:

Make the following actions to go with the song:

Text	Actions
Down in the forest	Hold hand to forehead as if looking out into the forest.
early in the morning,	Pretend to be yawning.
See the little Easter bunnies	Make bunny ears with hands on head.
all in a row.	Point to imaginary bunnies sitting in a row.
Eggs in their baskets	Make an egg shape with thumbs and index fingers. Then make large basket with arms.
brightly painted,	Make painting movement with one hand.
Ready, steady	Stamp feet twice.
(clap-clap-clap) –	Clap hands.
off they go.	Jump on the spot three times.

Games

Students will need hard-boiled eggs for all these activities.

Egg-shackling

Play this game in pairs.
Each player holds his/her egg firmly in one hand. The players then hit their eggs together.
The aim is to break the other player's egg, but keep your own egg intact. The winner keeps both eggs.

Egg-rolling

Play this game outdoors on a grassy slope.
All the players roll their eggs down a hill to see which egg can go the furthest without breaking. It used to be said that an egg that reached the bottom without breaking would bring good luck!

Egg-and-spoon race

This game is best played outdoors. Students will need a hard-boiled egg and a spoon.

1. All the racers line up with their eggs balanced on their spoons at arms length.
2. The starter says: "Ready, steady, go!"
3. On "go" the racers run to the finishing line (approx. 25 metres away) holding their eggs balanced on their spoons at arms length all the way. They must not touch the egg while it is on the spoon!

Make your own Easter table decoration

47

Students will need scissors, card, glue and coloured pencils (or equivalent) to make the table decorations. The illustrations on the worksheet are intended to be cut out and made into table decorations. Instructions are given on the worksheet.
Students can learn the poem, *Chook-Chook*, by heart and draw the hen and her family using the colours mentioned.

Hot cross buns

48

There is a recipe for Hot cross buns on this worksheet as well as a little background information about the buns and a well-known traditional poem.

Eggs, Eggs, Eggs

49

Students will need eggshell halves, a needle or pin, cotton, wool, glue, paint or coloured pencils (or equivalent) to make *egg monsters*. They will need eggshell halves, coloured pencils (or equivalent), cotton wool, water, cress seeds and plasticine to make *cress heads*.
Tell students to bring the dried eggshell halves with them to the lesson. (They will need to crack a fresh egg in half, wash the empty halves and let them dry.) If you are making Hot cross buns (copy master 48) they could use the eggshells from the eggs used in the recipe.

Solution to Easter egg hunt

There is an egg next to the front door.

- behind the sheep.
- on the tractor.
- in the dog's mouth.
- behind the car/in front of the gate.
- in the tree.
- under the daffodils.
- on the chimney.
- in the basket.
- next to/under the tree.
- in the car.

Easter in Britain

The Easter Bunnies

(words: trad./Wolfgang E. Hering/Brigitte Schanz-Hering;
music: traditional)

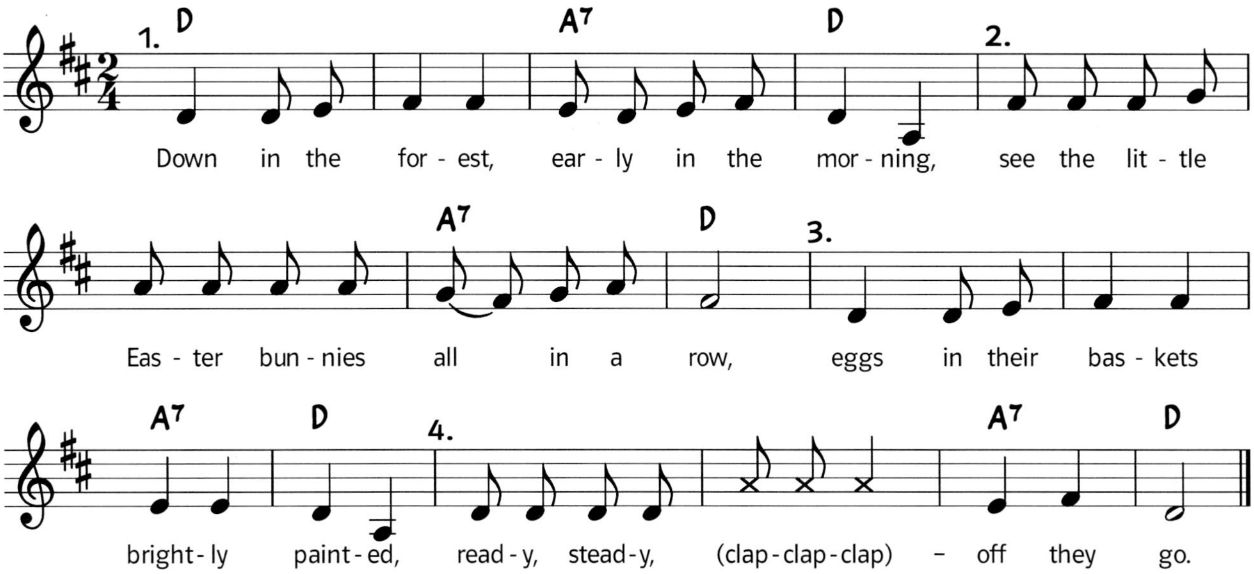

Down in the forest early in the morning,
See the little Easter bunnies all in a row,
Eggs in their baskets brightly painted,
Ready, steady (clap – clap – clap) – off they go.

Easter in Britain

The letters of the words have got mixed up. Can you write them properly?

papyH steEar!

— — — — — / — — — — — — !

atEsre gsge

— — — — — — / — — — —

tHo orssc snbu

— — — / — — — — — — / — — — —

geg-lolngri

— — — - — — — — — — —

geg-gnhkalcsi

— — — - — — — — — — — — —

sreEat nnuyb

— — — — — — / — — — — —

gge-nda-opons-erca

— — — - — — — - — — — — — - — — — —

ISBN 978-3-12-512751-7

Make your own Easter table decoration

1. *Colour in the Easter bunny and the chicks.*
2. *Stick them onto pieces of card.*
3. *Cut them out.*
4. *Fold back along the dotted lines to make them stand up.*

Chook-Chook

Chook, chook, chook-chook-chook!
Good morning, Mrs Hen.
How many chickens have you got?
Madam, I've got ten.
Four of them are yellow,
And four of them are brown,
And two of them are speckled red,
The nicest in the town.

(Mary Ann Hobermann)

You can also use the chicks to decorate hard-boiled eggs.

ISBN 978-3-12-512751-7

Hot cross buns

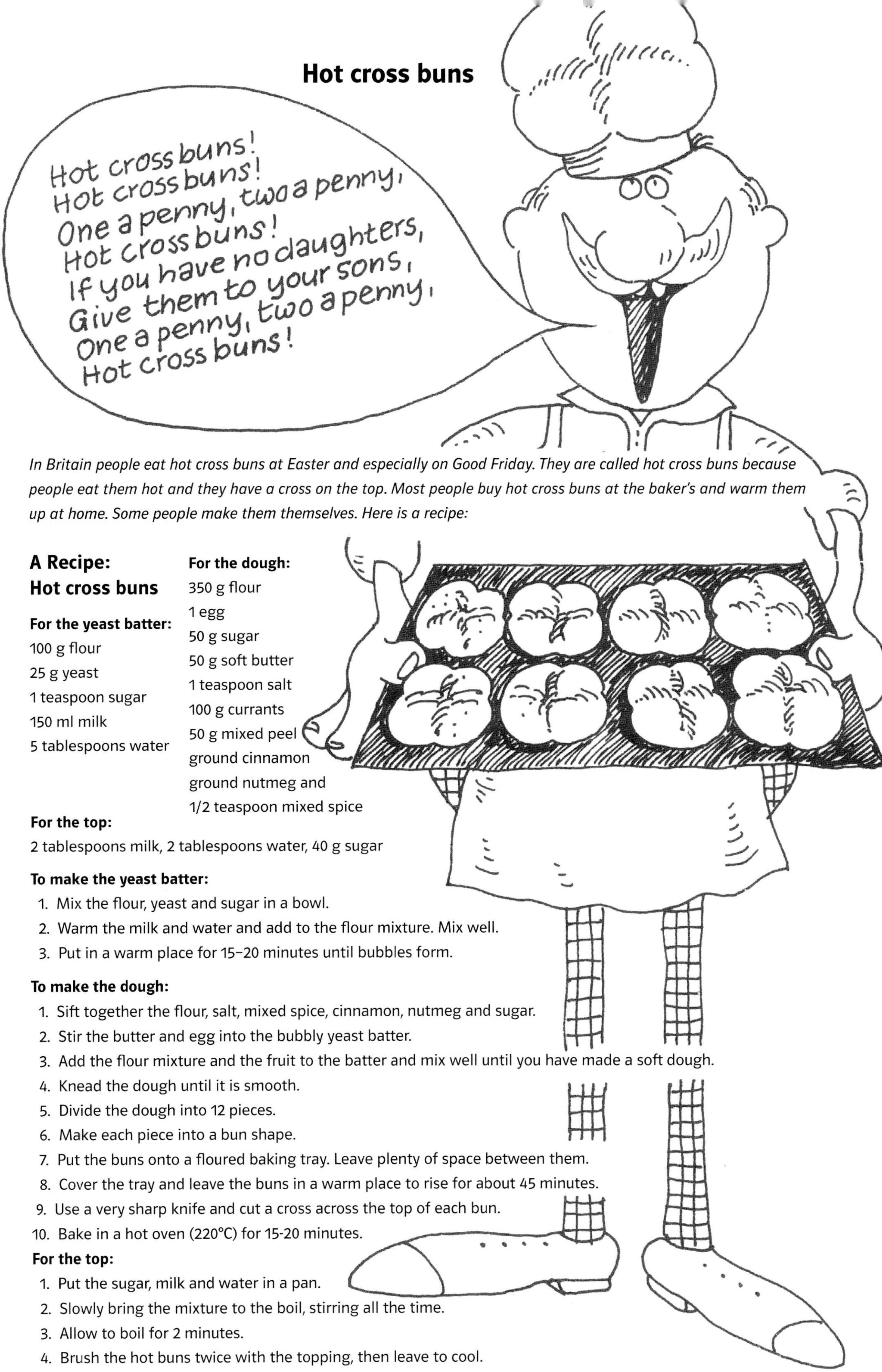

In Britain people eat hot cross buns at Easter and especially on Good Friday. They are called hot cross buns because people eat them hot and they have a cross on the top. Most people buy hot cross buns at the baker's and warm them up at home. Some people make them themselves. Here is a recipe:

A Recipe: Hot cross buns

For the yeast batter:
100 g flour
25 g yeast
1 teaspoon sugar
150 ml milk
5 tablespoons water

For the dough:
350 g flour
1 egg
50 g sugar
50 g soft butter
1 teaspoon salt
100 g currants
50 g mixed peel
ground cinnamon
ground nutmeg and
1/2 teaspoon mixed spice

For the top:
2 tablespoons milk, 2 tablespoons water, 40 g sugar

To make the yeast batter:

1. Mix the flour, yeast and sugar in a bowl.
2. Warm the milk and water and add to the flour mixture. Mix well.
3. Put in a warm place for 15–20 minutes until bubbles form.

To make the dough:

1. Sift together the flour, salt, mixed spice, cinnamon, nutmeg and sugar.
2. Stir the butter and egg into the bubbly yeast batter.
3. Add the flour mixture and the fruit to the batter and mix well until you have made a soft dough.
4. Knead the dough until it is smooth.
5. Divide the dough into 12 pieces.
6. Make each piece into a bun shape.
7. Put the buns onto a floured baking tray. Leave plenty of space between them.
8. Cover the tray and leave the buns in a warm place to rise for about 45 minutes.
9. Use a very sharp knife and cut a cross across the top of each bun.
10. Bake in a hot oven (220°C) for 15-20 minutes.

For the top:

1. Put the sugar, milk and water in a pan.
2. Slowly bring the mixture to the boil, stirring all the time.
3. Allow to boil for 2 minutes.
4. Brush the hot buns twice with the topping, then leave to cool.

ISBN 978-3-12-512751-7

Eggs, Eggs, Eggs …

Egg monsters and cress heads

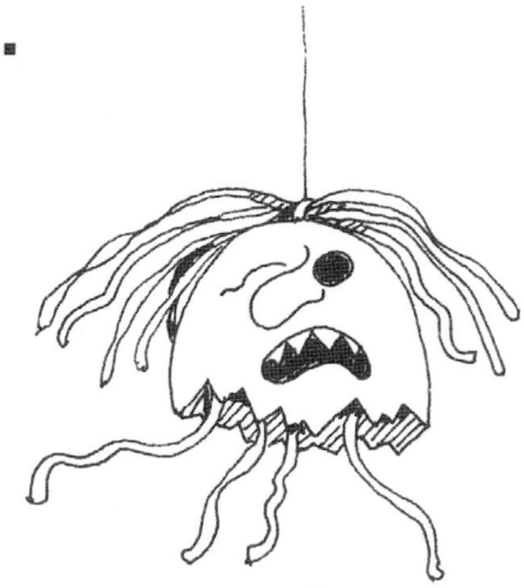

Carefully crack a fresh egg in half. Wash the empty shells and let them dry.

To make an egg monster:

1. Pierce a hole in the top of one eggshell half and thread a piece of cotton through it.
2. Knot the end of the cotton so that it cannot slip through the hole.
3. Paint a horrible face on the shell!
4. Stick some wool on for hair and legs.
5. Hang the egg monster from the ceiling or inside a door. Wait for the screams!

To make cress heads:

1. Paint faces on the eggshells as shown in the picture.
2. Put the egg faces on some plasticine, so they stand up.
3. Put some cotton wool inside the shells and wet it thoroughly.
4. Put cress seeds into the eggshells. It takes three or four days for the cress to grow.

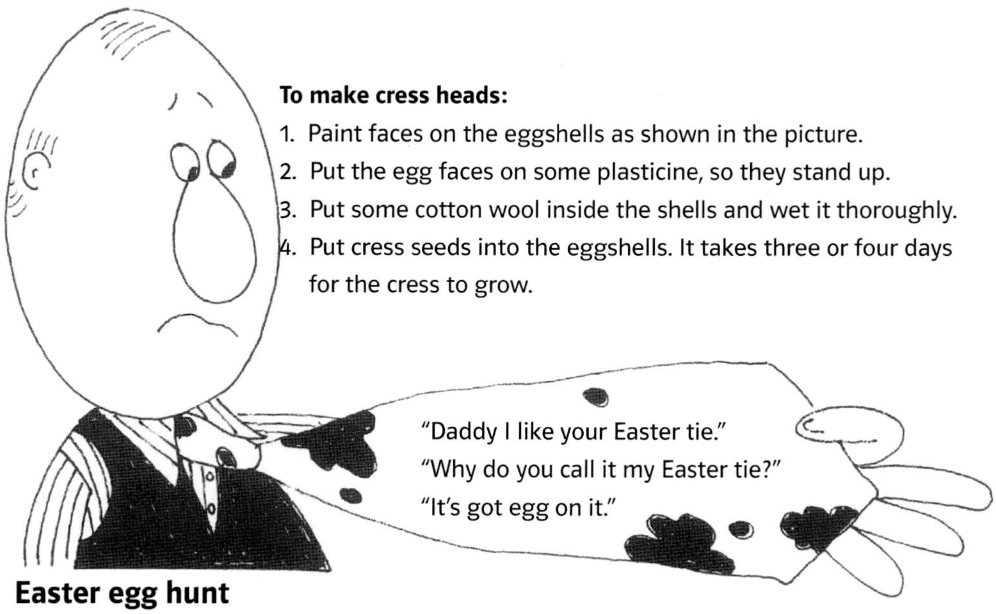

Easter egg hunt

There are eleven Easter eggs hidden in this picture. Can you find them? Write down where they are. Make sentences using on/under/behind/ in front of/in/next to …

Example:

There is an Easter egg next to the front door.

ISBN 978-3-12-512751-7

11 The merry month of May

The copy masters in this chapter are intended for use in May, or more broadly in late spring/early summer. They cover May Day and also May as a month for working in the garden.

May Morning

50

This is a lively and happy song which epitomises the atmosphere on a warm May Day (1st May) morning. It is the type of song which was probably sung when dancing around the May Pole (see below). When students are familiar with the words and the tune, you could divide them into groups of four or six and ask them to make up a dance to go with the song. They should pay attention to the text in the chorus and the second verse when they do this.
Some information about May Day in Britain, which could be copied and given to more able students, is given below. The information could also be given in the students' mother tongue.

May Day in Britain

For many centuries people all over Europe used to put up a May Pole on 1 May. It had flowers on the top and pretty ribbons dangling from it. People danced around it to the accompaniment of music or singing.
Nowadays in Britain you sometimes still see May Poles, usually in rural areas. However, May Day is not a public holiday. The 1st May is also known as "Labour Day", a day on which workers, usually in trade unions, traditionally hold demonstrations and rallies. The May Bank Holiday in Britain, which is a public holiday, is always the first Monday in May. This is often the first opportunity in the year to spend a long weekend outdoors. And so, on the Friday afternoon before the May Bank Holiday, there are almost always huge traffic jams on the motorways as everyone heads away from home. Some people head for the country, but the majority go in the direction of the seaside, which of course is (normally) easy to get to for everyone in Britain!

In the country

51

Students will need scissors, glue and coloured pencils (or equivalent).
This exercise can be used to learn or practise the names of farm animals and birds.

In my garden

53

This worksheet practises the names for flowers (in the poem), and the names for herbs, vegetables and colours (in the picture). Students will need coloured pencils (or equivalent).

In my garden: Make sure the students know the names of all the flowers mentioned in the poem before reading it to them. Then divide the class into six groups, one for each of the first six verses of the poem. Each group reads the first three lines of their verse, then all students join in with the last (counting) line. In the last verse each group reads the line (s) in which their flower is mentioned: group 1 – line 1; group 2 – line 2; group 3 – line 5; group 4 – lines 3 & 4; group 5 – line 6; group 6 – line 7. All the students read the last line in unison. Students can then draw pictures of their verses and write the words underneath. Use the finished pictures to decorate the classroom.

Herbs and Vegetables: make sure students are familiar with the names of the herbs and vegetables in the picture before asking them to complete the tasks.

Additional exercise: If your school has a school garden why not have an English corner in it? Grow plants, e. g. herbs, flowers and vegetables, and write their English names on the labels. (Make your own labels out of cardboard covered in self-adhesive plastic.)

Make your own wormery

53

Ask students to do this "experiment" at school or at home! The instructions and the things they will need are all on the worksheet!

Draw a Spring Picture

16

As in the autumn and winter chapters, this exercise closes the chapter on spring and allows students to show that they are familiar with spring vocabulary. Use the pictures to decorate the classroom.

First have the students complete the heading of the picture, then give the students the following instructions. Before or while you read out the instructions, you may write the important vocabulary on the blackboard or overhead projector.

Draw a spring picture and colour it in. Draw
- people dancing around a May Pole on the right-hand side of the river. They are holding ribbons dangling from the May Pole in their hands;
- a basket with Easter eggs and an Easter bunny in the bottom right-hand corner of the picture;
- sheep and daffodils on the hill on the right;
- a blossoming tree with a bird's nest in it on the left-hand side of the house;
- a meadow with tulips, pansies and daisies in it in front of the house;
- blue sky;
- the sun shining brightly.

May Morning

(words and music: traditional)

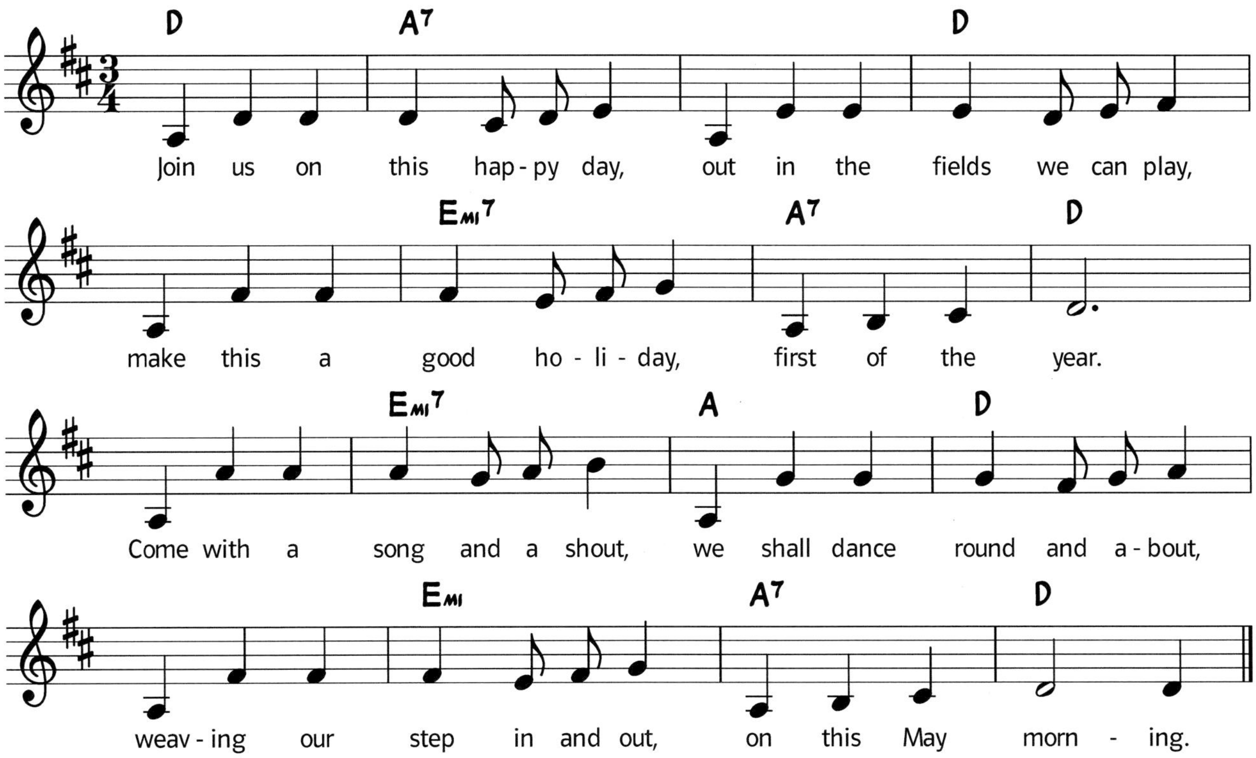

1. Join us on this happy day,
   Out in the fields we can play,
   Make this a good holiday,
   First of the year.

Chorus:
   Come with a song and a shout,
   We shall dance round and about,
   Weaving our step in and out,
   On this May morning.

2. Come show us how you can sing,
   Join hands and dance in a ring,
   We say hello to the spring,
   First of the year.

Chorus:
   Come with a song and a shout,
   We shall dance round and about,
   Weaving our step in and out,
   On this May morning.

ISBN 978-3-12-512751-7

In the country

Colour the animals and the picture. Then cut out the animals and stick them onto the picture in the correct places.

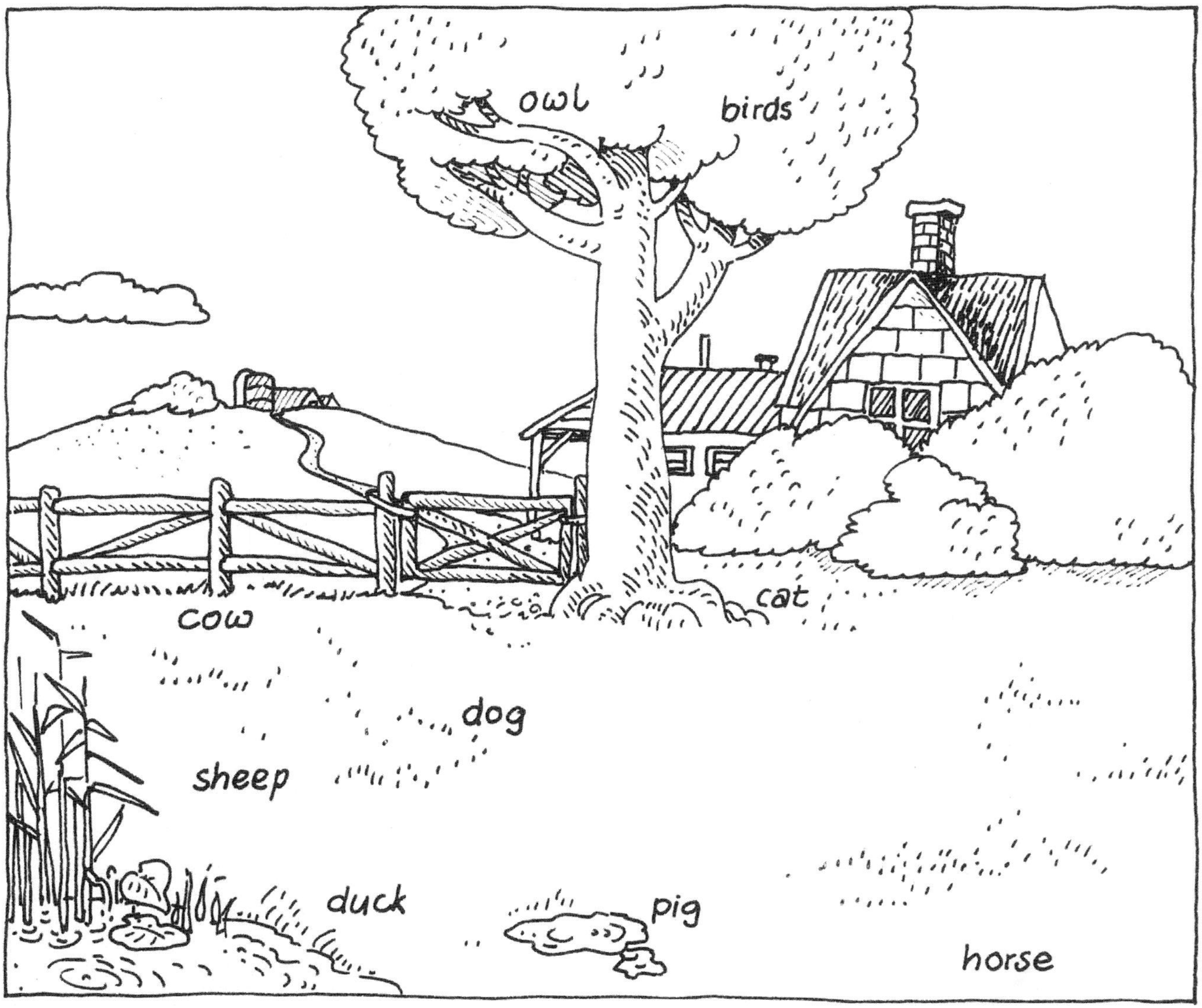

ISBN 978-3-12-512751-7

In my garden

In my garden

In my little garden
By the apple tree,
Daffodils are dancing –
One – two – three!

In my little garden
By the kitchen door,
Daisies red are smiling –
Two – three – four!

In my little garden
By the winding drive,
Roses bright are climbing –
Three – four – five!

In my little garden
By the pile of bricks,
Hollyhocks are growing –
Four – five – six!

In my little garden
Down in sunny Devon,
Violets are hiding –
Five – six – seven!

In my little garden
By the cottage gate,
Pansies gay are shining –
Six – seven – eight!

Daffodils in golden gowns,
Daisies all in red,
Hollyhocks so very tall
By the garden shed,
Roses in the sunshine,
Violets dewy bright,
Pansies smiling gaily –
hat a lovely sight!

Herbs and Vegetables

How does the caterpillar get to the lettuce? Show him the way.
After you have found the way through the maze you can colour the picture in.

Write the names of the herbs and vegetables.

lettuce
radishes
chives
parsley
cucumber
carrots
onions
peas
beans
tomatoes

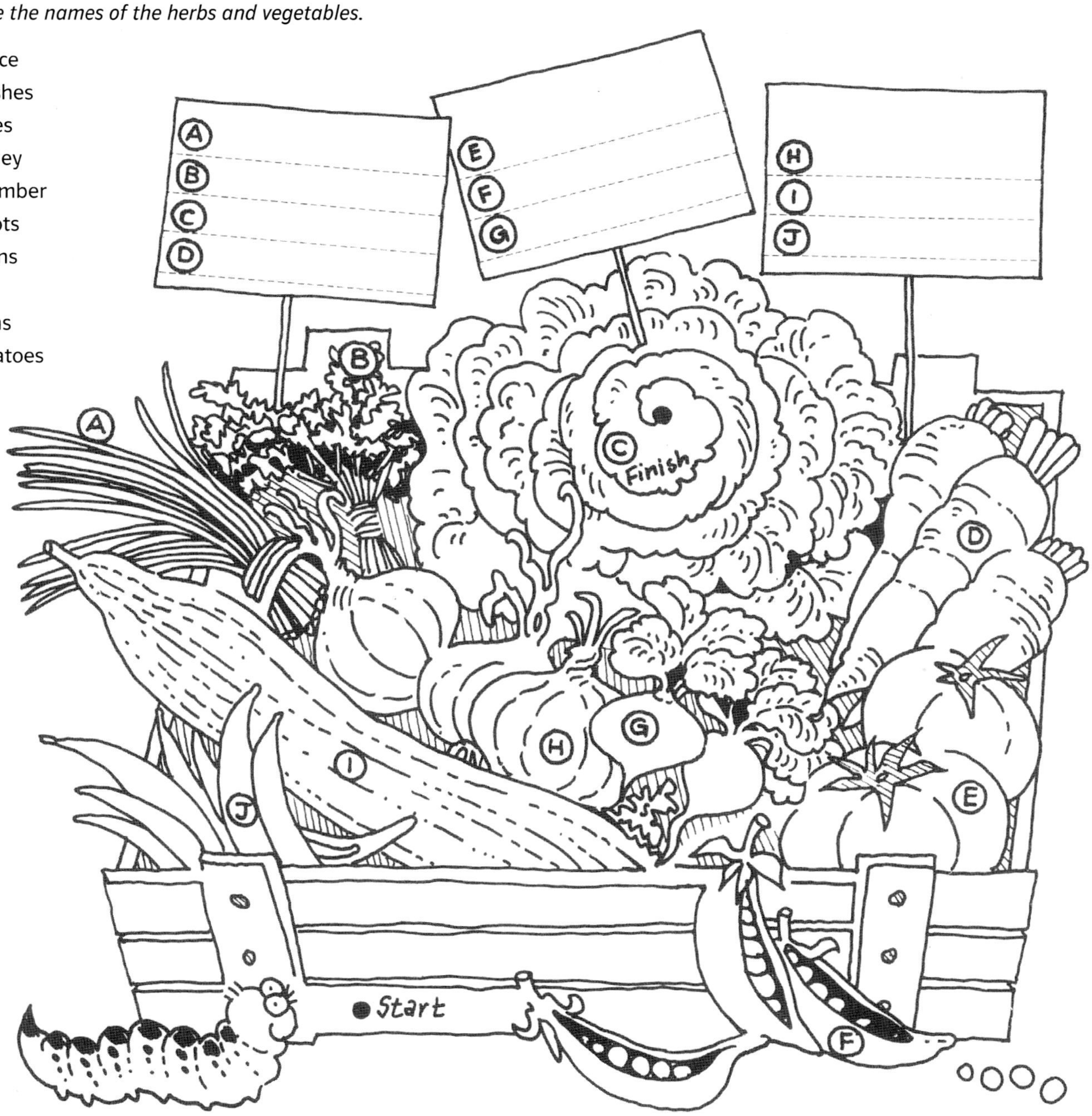

ISBN 978-3-12-512751-7

Make your own Wormery

You will need: a jar, some earth, some sand, a bottle, some leaves, two or three worms, some dark paper, some water.

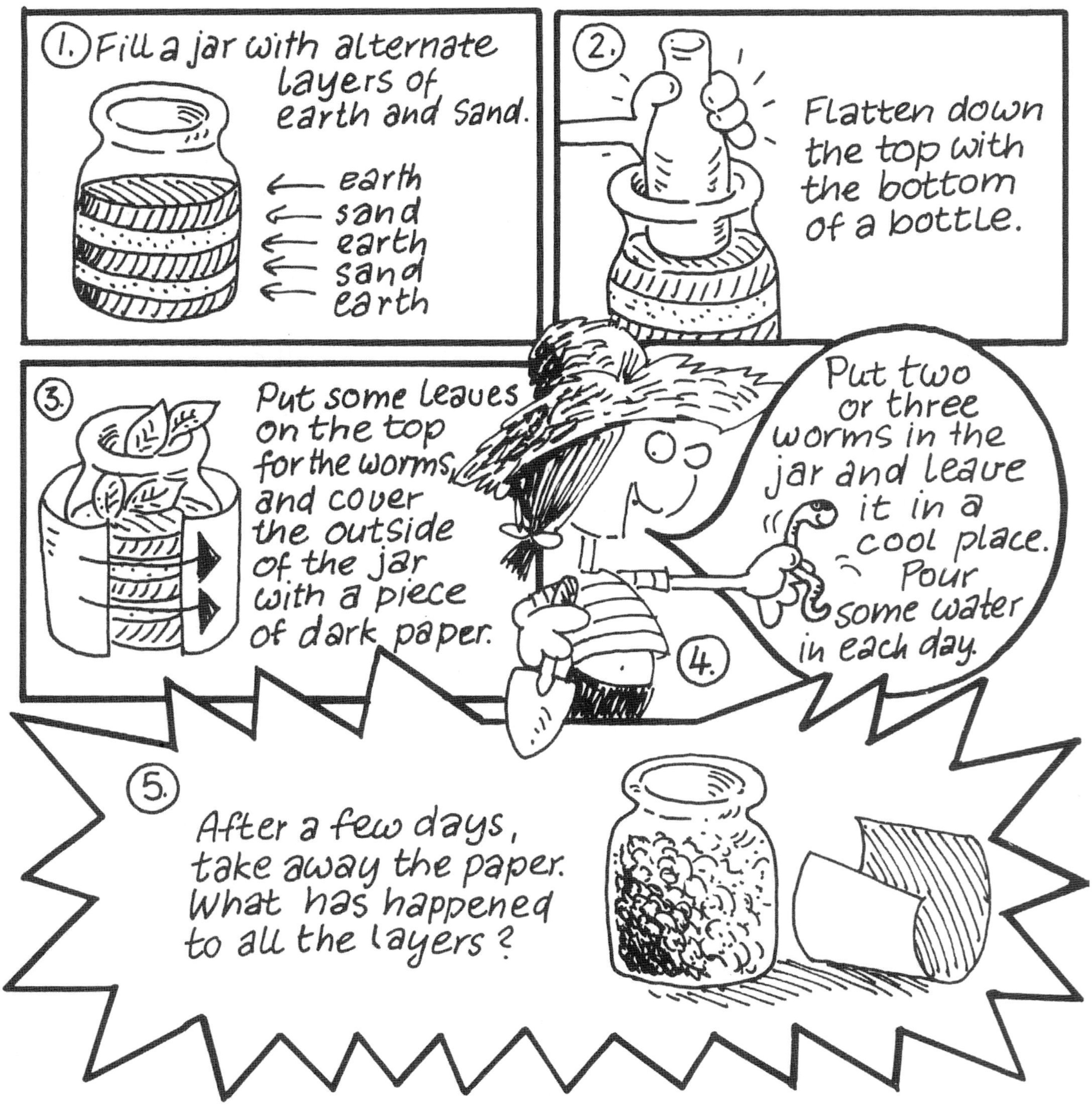

ISBN 978-3-12-512751-7

12 Happy Birthday!

This chapter includes a variety of activities connected with birthdays. They can be used whenever it is a student's birthday.
All students are pleased when their birthday is remembered in class so at the beginning of the school year you might like to make a class wall-calendar (see page 46) and fill in all the students' birthdays. This provides a good opportunity to practise dates and months, and means that both the teacher and students can see at a glance whose birthday is coming next.

Happy Birthday

54

This is a special birthday song.
The introduction and the ending of the song can be sung by the teacher or all the students together. Divide the class into three groups for the rest of the song: one for each of the three verses. All the students sing the chorus. All the students should "click", "clap" and "stamp" as indicated in each verse.

The Bumps

Students might like to give the person whose birthday it is "the bumps". This is a tradition in Britain, especially amongst children. The person whose birthday it is lies on the floor. Six (or more) children and adults stand around him/her and take hold of his/her legs, arms, body, etc. The person is then swung (but not thrown!) up into the air and back down to the ground, once for each year of her/his age and once for luck! Each time the person goes up all the "lifters" call out the number. (One – two – three, etc.). On the last lift they call out: "And one for luck!"

Party Time

55

Students will need coloured pencils (or equivalent), card and glue.

A Giant's Cake: When students are familiar with the text of the poem they can draw a picture of the cake as it is described in the poem. You could point out to students that it is customary in Britain to have a cake decorated with icing and with candles on the top. There is always one more candle than the age of the person – the extra one is for luck!

Make your own party place cards: These place cards can also be used for other types of parties, e. g. for a class party.
The teacher should read the instructions through once with the whole class. A few days before a student's birthday the teacher can give the student some copies of the copy master so that she/he can make place cards for her/ his birthday party in time.

Two Recipes: Sweets

56

The ingredients and instructions are all on the worksheet. Students can make the sweets either in the school kitchen or at home. They could also make trifle as a party dessert (see copy master 22).

Party Games

These games can be played at home or in the classroom. Students can play in small groups or all together.

Kippers

Explain what kippers are to students before starting the game. Better still, bring a kipper with you! Of course, you can play the game using other words which may be amusing for students, e.g. sausage.

1. Use the choosing rhyme (see page 5) to decide who will be "it".
2. Now the other students ask the one who is "it" questions. For example: "What have you got on your head?" or "What do you smell of?" or "What does our teacher smell of?"!
3. No matter what is asked the person who is "it" must answer "Kippers" without smiling.
4. If the person who is "it" smiles, then the questioner becomes "it" in a new round.

Fly away, Robin

Before playing the game ask students to name things that can fly and write the words on the board (e. g. bird, sparrow, butterfly, aeroplane, cuckoo, fly, bee, bumble bee, moth, helicopter, witch, etc.).

1. Either the person whose birthday it is, or another student is the caller.
2. Students sit around a table with both hands on the table top.
3. The caller says: "Fly away," and then gives the name of a creature or thing that either can or can't fly.
4. Players raise their hands high in the air when something is called that can fly, but keep them on the table if something is mentioned which can't fly.
5. If a player makes the wrong action they are out.
6. The last person left in is the caller in the next game.

Vampires – see page 24

I sent a letter to my love – see page 61

Egg-and-spoon race – see page 81

Happy Birthday

(words and music: Robert Metcalf)

Whose birthday is it today?
Here's a song for you:

Chorus:

Happy birthday, many happy returns,
Happy birthday, many happy returns,
Happy birthday, many happy returns, of the day
To you!

1. Our fingers click away (click, click)
   Wishing you a lovely day. (click, click)
   and especially for you
   Here's a birthday song:

   Chorus

2. Our hands are clapping, too, (clap, clap)
   And they know just what to do. (clap, clap)
   And especially for you
   Here's a birthday song:

   Chorus

3. Hear the stamping of our feet, (stamp, stamp)
   It's you they wish to greet, (stamp, stamp)
   And especially for you
   Here's a birthday song:

   Chorus

Whose birthday is it today?
That was a song for you.

ISBN 978-3-12-512751-7

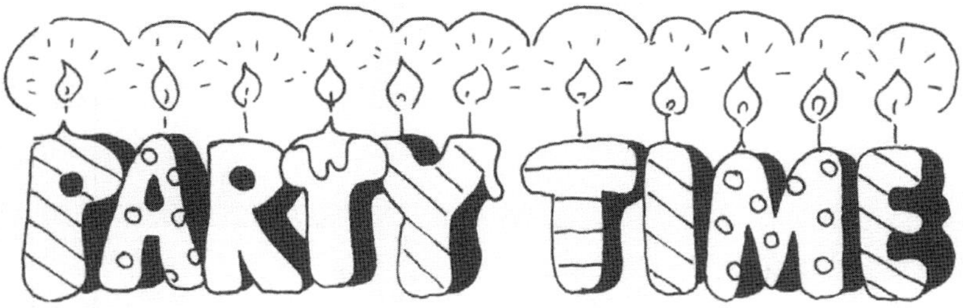

A Giant's Cake

Each year I have a birthday,
When people buy me toys,
And mother gives a party
To lots of girls and boys.

I have a cake with candles,
And icing, pink and white,
With rosy candles lighted,
It makes a lovely sight.

Each year the cake grows larger,
Another light to take,
So if I grow much older
I'll need a giant's cake.

(Evelina San Garde)

Make your own party place cards

1. Colour the cards.
2. Write one guest's name on each place card.
3. Stick the cards onto a piece of card.
4. Cut out the cards and fold back the tabs along the dotted lines.
5. Put a card at each guest's place at the table.

(Do not forget to write your own name on a card!)

ISBN 978-3-12-512751-7

Two Recipes: Sweets

Here are two recipes for some sweets. You can serve them at parties.

Coconut Ice

1 kg caster sugar
125 ml milk
30 g butter
230 g desiccated coconut
pink food colouring

1. Put the sugar, butter and milk into a saucepan and bring slowly to the boil stirring all the time to dissolve the sugar.
2. Boil for four minutes whilst still stirring.
3. Remove the mixture from the heat, add the coconut and stir well.
4. Pour half the mixture into a greased tin which should not be too deep (about 4 cms). Let this cool a little. Colour the other half pink and pour on top.
5. Cut into squares when cool.

Chocolate Fudge

1 kg brown sugar
125 ml milk
250 g butter
3 tablespoons chocolate
grated rind and juice of an orange
a few drops of vanilla essence

1. Put the sugar and milk into a soucepan and leave for one hour.
2. Add the butter and chocolate, and the rind and juice of the orange.
3. Bring to the boil slowly. Boil fast for about 12 minutes. The mixture will rise in the saucepan.
4. Remove from heat when the mixture begins to sink. Leave to stand for 2 minutes, then add the vanilla essence and beat with a wooden spoon until the mixture thickens.
5. Pour into a greased tin and allow to cool. Cut into little squares or rectangles when cool.

ISBN 978-3-12-512751-7

13 No more pencils, no more books!

This final chapter brings the school year to a close. There are lots of "fun" things to do and songs to sing. Particular attention is paid to the fact that students often go on outings at this time of year (e.g. to the zoo), that the weather is often good so students spend time outdoors doing sports, and, last but not least, that they are looking forward to the long summer holidays.

Muscles

57

The words in this song should not be taken too seriously! Students can act out the various activities mentioned. In large classes each activity can be assigned to a single student. There are 14 people doing things in the song (as well as Katy's mates in verse 4), so that 18-20 students can take part. In smaller classes one student can take more than one role. One student – a very sporty one! – could even act out all the activities.
Play the CD for the verses or ask a group of students to sing them.
Everybody should sing the chorus and do the following actions:

Text	Action
Muscles must be hard, kids,	Raise arms as if showing off big muscles.
Shouldn't melt like lard, kids,	Let arms hang limply.
Muscles must be really hard,	Raise arms again to show off big muscles.
Not made of lard, not made of lard.	Let arms hang limply again.

Sports Puzzle

58

This puzzle can also be used when the words for various sports are being learnt. To make the puzzle a little easier and also if some of the words are new to students, the teacher could write all the words on the board first and then set a time limit for finding them.
Another possibility would be to copy the puzzle onto a transparency and present it to students via the overhead projector. Divide the class into teams (groups of four). Each team takes it in turn to come and circle one word. They have ten seconds each time to do this. (The other students in the class can count out the ten seconds in unison. Beware: this may create a lot of noise in the classroom!) The team which finds the most words is the winner.

B	O	X	I	N	G	H	S	A	U	Q	S	T	R	A	D	C
A	B	A	S	K	E	T	B	A	L	L	B	F	E	S	D	R
I	G	R	I	C	E	-	S	K	A	T	I	N	G	I	C	O
F	H	C	K	A	L	M	A	S	W	I	M	M	I	N	G	Q
I	Q	H	P	N	C	R	I	C	K	E	T	N	O	N	Y	U
S	S	E	R	O	S	T	L	U	G	O	L	F	G	E	M	E
H	O	R	S	E	-	R	I	D	I	N	G	O	N	T	N	T
I	C	Y	X	I	Y	W	N	H	J	U	D	O	I	-	A	L
N	C	Z	D	N	C	B	G	O	L	F	A	T	B	E	S	L
G	E	R	U	G	B	Y	E	C	O	N	F	B	M	L	T	A
K	R	I	H	G	N	I	I	K	S	L	M	A	I	B	I	B
B	O	W	L	I	N	G	N	E	T	B	A	L	L	A	C	E
O	P	G	V	O	L	L	E	Y	B	A	L	L	C	T	S	S
G	N	I	T	A	K	S	-	R	E	L	L	O	R	T	U	A
C	Y	C	L	I	N	G	W	N	O	T	N	I	M	D	A	B

Solution

archery, badminton, baseball, basketball, bowling, boxing, canoeing, climbing, cricket, croquet, cycling, darts, fishing, football, golf, gymnastics, hockey, horse-riding, ice-skating, judo, netball, roller-skating, rugby, sailing, skiing, soccer, squash, swimming, table tennis, tennis, volleyball

Zoo Picture Crossword

59

This crossword practises the names of zoo animals. Make sure students are familiar with them before giving them the crossword to do. It is a good exercise to do before singing the song *To-do at the Zoo* (copy master 60). When students have completed the crossword ask them about any visits they have made to the zoo, e. g. find out what their favourite animals are and why, which animal they would most like to see that they have never seen, etc.

Solution

across	**down**
1. zebra	2. ape
3. elephant	4. tiger
6. rhinoceros	5. crocodile
8. kangaroo	7. snake
10. camel	9. giraffe
11. donkey	12. lion

To-do at the Zoo

60

This is a joke song about a very special – and funny – zoo. The text is quite difficult, so the teacher will need to explain new vocabulary, etc., before introducing the song. The *Zoo Picture Crossword* (copy master 59) is an ideal introduction to the topic. The song could just be listened to by the class.
To sing the song, divide the class into six groups, one for each verse. If the class is big enough the third verse, which is twice as long as the others, could be sung by two groups making seven groups altogether. The chorus is sung by the whole class.
Practise the words in the rhythm of the song without the music first.
Students can draw pictures of the different scenes described in the song. Decorate the classroom with the pictures. As the song is being sung or listened to ask students to point to the appropriate pictures on the wall. Copy master 61 is a comprehension exercise based on the song.

To-do at the Zoo: Worksheet

61

This is a comprehension exercise to go with the song on copy master 60.

Solution

(1) giraffe, (2) elephant, (3) dentist, (4) painter, (5) lion, (6) ape, (7) zoo director, (8) zebra, (9) crocodile, (10) camel, (11) rhinoceros, (12) pink flamingos, (13) kangaroo, (14) lioness

Game

Round the world

This game practises the names of towns, cities and countries. *Round the World* is actually a car game, so it could be played on long coach rides. Of course, it can also be played in the classroom.

1. *On a journey:* One of the students calls out a place name which they have seen on a signpost, e. g. Dartford.
   In the classroom: One student (chosen using the choosing rhyme, see page 8) decides on a place name and calls it out.
2. The other students call out in turn and as quickly as possible a town, city or country beginning with the letters of the place name in the correct order. (The English pronounciation of the names of towns, countries or cities should be used.) e. g. Dartford: Denmark – Amsterdam – Rochester – Tokyo – Finland – Oxford – Rome – Dublin.
3. If a student can't think of a name they are out and the next student continues.

Variation:
The object of the game is to see which student can stay at the front the longest:

1. Put two chairs at the front of the class and choose two students (via a choosing rhyme) to sit on them.
2. Call out the name of a town.
3. The two students take it in turns to say the name of a town, city or country as above. Limit the time they have to do so (e.g. three seconds – the other students can count out the seconds in unison).
4. If the students get to the end of the word, quickly give them another.
5. When a student fails to think of a word, she/he leaves the seat and chooses another student to follow her/him.

62

Baggage Claim

This is a simple game for two players. Each pair needs a dice and two counters. It is ideal for playing on the last day of term. It is just for fun!

63

At the seaside

Students will need coloured pencils (or equivalent).
In Britain nobody lives very far from the sea, so the seaside is a popular holiday destination. Whereas in many parts of central Europe some students may never have visited the sea, almost all British children will have been to the coast before they are more than a couple of years old.
There are some poems and tongue twisters on this copy master, which students should enjoy practising. There is also a scene to be coloured by numbers.

Draw a Summer Picture

Students will need coloured pencils (or equivalent).
This is the last in the set of seasonal pictures.

First have the students complete the heading of the picture, then give the students the following instructions. Before or while you read out the instructions, you may write the important vocabulary on the blackboard or overhead projector.

Draw a summer picture and colour it in. Draw
- children playing in the river;
- a family, with a dog, having a picnic in the bottom right-hand side of the picture;
- a tree covered in green leaves on the left-hand side of the house;
- a cat sleeping under the tree;
- some people riding bikes on the hill behind the house;
- a man and a woman sunbathing next to the house;
- the sun shining brightly.

Holiday

64 & 65

This song has been specially written for the last day of the school year.
Encourage the students to accompany the song on percussion instruments, e. g. bongo drums, rattles, clappers, maracas, guiros, and create a real holiday atmosphere in the classroom! The chorus can be sung in three voices as shown on copy master 65.

Muscles

(words and music: Bernhard Hering/Wolfgang E. Hering/Bernd Meyerholz;
translation: Robert Metcalf/Brigitte Schanz- Hering)

1. Skinny Alexander
   Plays with his chest expander,
   And little Josephine
   Bounces on the trampoline.
   And when I'm in the P. E. class
   I leap and skip and run so fast
   That even Dad – it's plain to see –
   Gets tired out just watching me.

Chorus:

Muscles must be hard, kids,
Shouldn't melt like lard, kids,
Muscles must be really hard,
Not made of lard,
Not made of lard.

2. Shy and timid Ludo
   Practises his judo,
   Pale and weedy Marty
   Tries to do karate.
   And one thing makes me really laugh –
   Susan swimming in the bath.
   She dives down under for a while
   And comes up with a toothy smile.

Chorus

3. The only sport for Dennis
   Is obviously tennis,
   While his younger sister Pat
   Can't sleep without her ping-pong bat.
   And every day at six o'clock
   Judy jogs around the block,
   So early in the morning
   When you and I are yawning.

Chorus

4. My nextdoor neighbour Jane
   Plays football even in the rain.
   Whizzing down the road goes Mike
   On his rusty, squeeky trike.
   Cheeky Katy and her mates
   Rush around on roller skates,
   And even old Aunt Kitty
   Skates through the city.

Chorus

ISBN 978-3-12-512751-7

Sports Puzzle

There are more than 28 different kinds of sports in this word square. Can you find them? The first one has been done for you.

↑↓ ⇉

B	O	X	I	N	G	H	S	A	U	Q	S	T	R	A	D	C
A	B	A	S	K	E	T	B	A	L	L	B	F	E	S	D	R
I	G	R	I	C	E	–	S	K	A	T	I	N	G	I	C	O
F	H	C	K	A	L	M	A	S	W	I	M	M	I	N	G	Q
I	Q	H	P	N	C	R	I	C	K	E	T	N	O	N	Y	U
S	S	E	R	O	S	T	L	U	G	O	L	F	G	E	M	E
H	O	R	S	E	–	R	I	D	I	N	G	O	N	T	N	T
I	C	Y	X	I	Y	W	N	H	J	U	D	O	I	V	A	L
N	C	Z	D	N	C	B	G	O	L	F	A	T	B	E	S	L
G	E	R	U	G	B	Y	E	C	O	N	F	B	M	L	T	A
K	R	I	H	G	N	I	I	K	S	L	M	A	I	B	I	B
B	O	W	L	I	N	G	N	E	T	B	A	L	L	A	C	E
Q	P	G	V	O	L	L	E	Y	B	A	L	L	C	T	S	S
G	N	I	T	A	K	S	–	R	E	L	L	O	R	T	U	A
C	Y	C	L	I	N	G	W	N	O	T	N	I	M	D	A	B

golf

Your score

over 28 = excellent

22 – 28 = good

12 – 21 = fair

ISBN 978-3-12-512751-7

Zoo Picture Crossword

ISBN 978-3-12-512751-7

To-do at the Zoo

(words and music: Bernhard Hering/Wolfgang E. Hering/
Bernd Meyerholz; translation: Robert Metcalf)

Chorus:
What a to-do at the zoo!
What a to-do at the zoo!

1. Last Sunday morning we walked down to the zoo.
   A camel at the entrance charged us ten pounds twenty-two.
   Was this all for publicity or just a hoax?
   And then an ape came up to us and started telling jokes.

   Chorus

2. A zebra had just had a bath clearly much too hot.
   His stripes had melted all away, but he just said, "So what?
   I'll simply call the painter up." And he came –
   And in ten minutes painted on that zebra's stripes again.

   Chorus

3. A rhinoceros with toothache was crying out in pain.
   A dentist came and with the help of an enormous crane
   Performed an operation, and when that was done
   The rhino said: "Oh, thanks a lot, I found that rather fun!"
   Just round the corner sat an elephant in tears.
   I asked him what the matter was and he said, "Oh, for years
   I've tried so hard to diet, but I'm such a funk.
   I always keep a bar of chocolate hidden up my trunk."

   Chorus

4. A hairdresser was cutting off the lion's mighty mane
   The lioness said, "Leo, darling, are you quite insane?"
   He now looked rather silly, hardly dangerous.
   But when he roared he scared the living daylights out of us.

   Chorus

5. Down at the duck pond a dance was under way.
   The Pink Flamingo Rock Band had just started to play.
   An old giraffe was dancing with a kangaroo
   Who said, "I haven't danced like this since 1982!"

   Chorus

6. The zoo director's office was just like the zoo.
   Two monkeys danced upon the desk with a noisy gnu.
   A crocodile sat reading in a bowler hat.
   We thought it time to go back home – we'd had enough of that!

   Chorus

ISBN 978-3-12-512751-7

To-do at the Zoo: Worksheet

1. Who says or thinks what? Write the names next to the bubbles.

2. Now draw a picture of your favourite scene using the text in the bubbles. Put your pictures on the wall in your classroom and make a "crazy zoo"!

Oh no, fifty kilos heavier than last week!

A great dancer, this kangaroo!

(1) ______________________________

My first operation with the help of a crane.

(2) ______________________________

(3) ______________________________

I'd like to have my mane cut.

Had your bath too hot again?!

(5) ______________________________

(4) ______________________________

What are these monkeys doing in my office?

(7) ______________________________

Do you know this one? Fifty monkeys were travelling …

(9) ______________________________

What a funny book!

(6) ______________________________

Oh no, not My stripes …!

(8) ______________________________

Ouch!!!

Ten pounds twenty-two, please.

(11) ______________________________

(10) ______________________________

Yeah, yeah, yeah!

(12) ______________________________

(14) ______________________________

My best dance since 1982.

Are you crazy, Leo?

(13) ______________________________

ISBN 978-3-12-512751-7

Baggage Claim

A game for two players

You need a dice and two counters.
One player plays on the "Singapore belt", the other one on the "London belt". Who will be the first to get their baggage?

1. *Put your counter on "Start".*
2. *Throw the dice and move the number of squares shown on the dice.*
3. *If you land on a square with a suitcase on it, you have collected it. Put a tick ☑ in the box.*
4. *The one who is the first to collect all their suitcases is the winner.*

Suitcases collected	Player A	Player B
1		
2		
3		
4		
5		

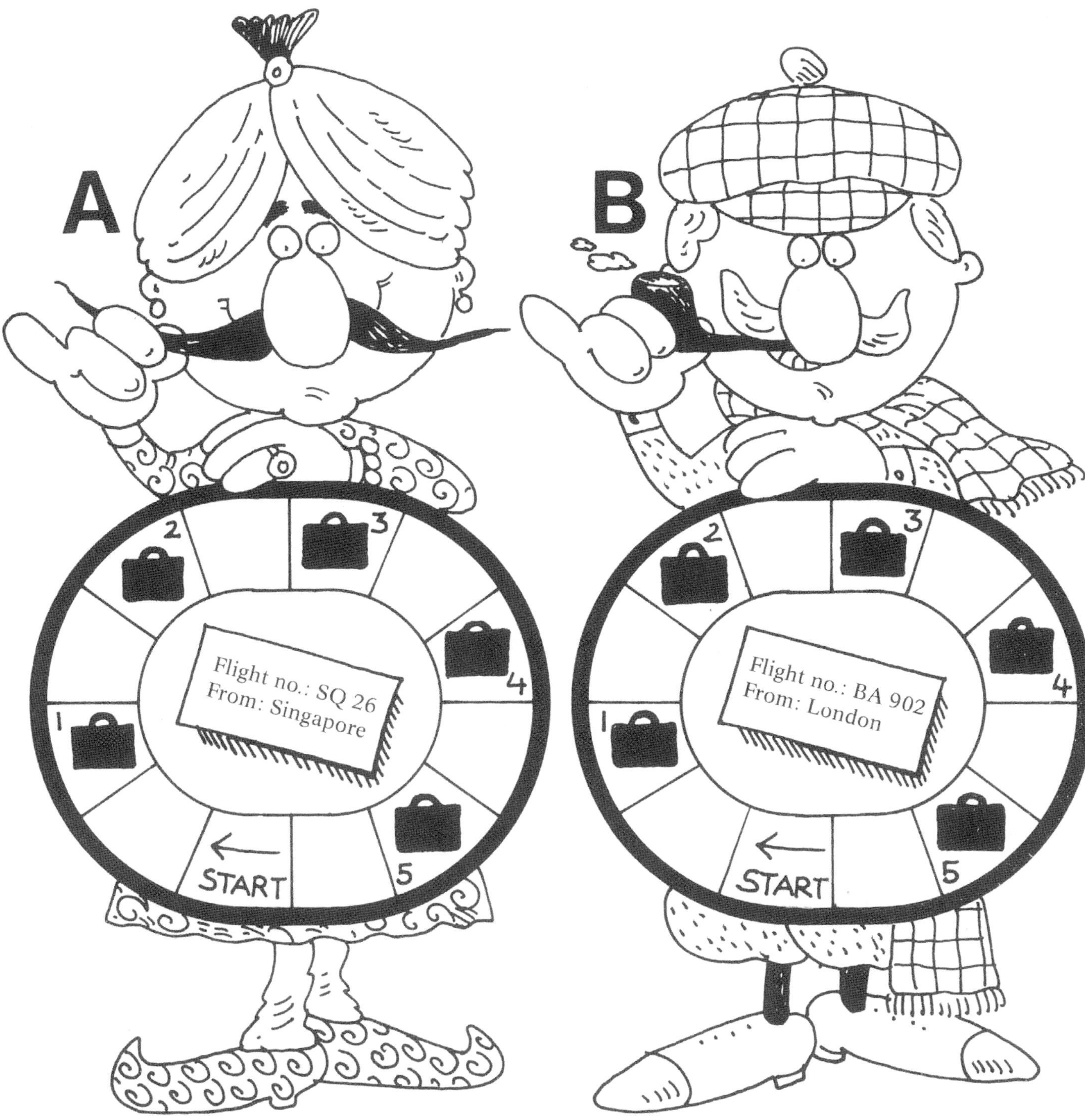

ISBN 978-3-12-512751-7

At the seaside

Sea Poems

There are big waves

There are big waves and little waves
Green waves and blue.
Waves you can jump over,
Waves you can dive through,
Waves that rise up
Like a great water wall,
Waves that swell softly
And don't break at all,
Waves that can whisper,
Waves that can roar,
And tiny waves that run at you
Running on the shore.

(Eleanor Farjeon)

Shell Secrets

Tell me your secrets, pretty shell,
I will promise not to tell!
Humming, humming, soft and low –
ll about the sea, I know.
You are murmuring, I think,
Of the sea-weeds, green and pink.
Of the tiny baby shells
Where the mother mermaid dwells.
Pretty shell, I'm waiting here,
Come, and whisper in my ear.

Tongue Twisters

Swan, swim over the sea
Swim, swan, swim.
Swan, swim, back again,
Well swum, swan.

She sells sea shells
On the seashore.

A picture postcard

Colour the picture by numbers.

1 = blue
2 = red
3 = yellow
4 = green
5 = black
6 = brown

ISBN 978-3-12-512751-7

Holiday

(words: trad./Wolfgang E. Hering/Brigitte Schanz-Hering;
music: Bernhard Hering)

1. No more pencils, no more books
   No more teachers' ugly looks.
   Ev'rything will be OK,
   Tomorrow we're on holiday.

Chorus:

Holiday, holiday, holiday, holiday,
Holiday, holiday, holiday.

2. No more Latin, no more French,
   No more sitting on a hard school bench,
   No more English, no more stick,
   No more flippin' arithmetic.

3. No more blackboard, no more chalk,
   No more teachers' crazy talk,
   Days just full of joy and fun,
   We can play out in the sun.

Chorus

4. No more lessons, no more hell
   No more lists of words to spell
   When the bell begins to ring,
   Ev'ryone will start to sing.

Chorus (twice)

ISBN 978-3-12-512751-7

Holiday: Chorus for three voices

ISBN 978-3-12-512751-7

Guitar Chord Diagrams

Here are all the guitar chords you will need in order to play the songs in this book.
The numbers refer to the fingertips which are used to press down the strings on the fret (1 = index finger,2 = middle finger, 3 = ring finger, 4 = little finger).
Only those strings which have a circle or a number in the chord diagram can be played.
The double line in the chord diagram refers to the root note of the chord.

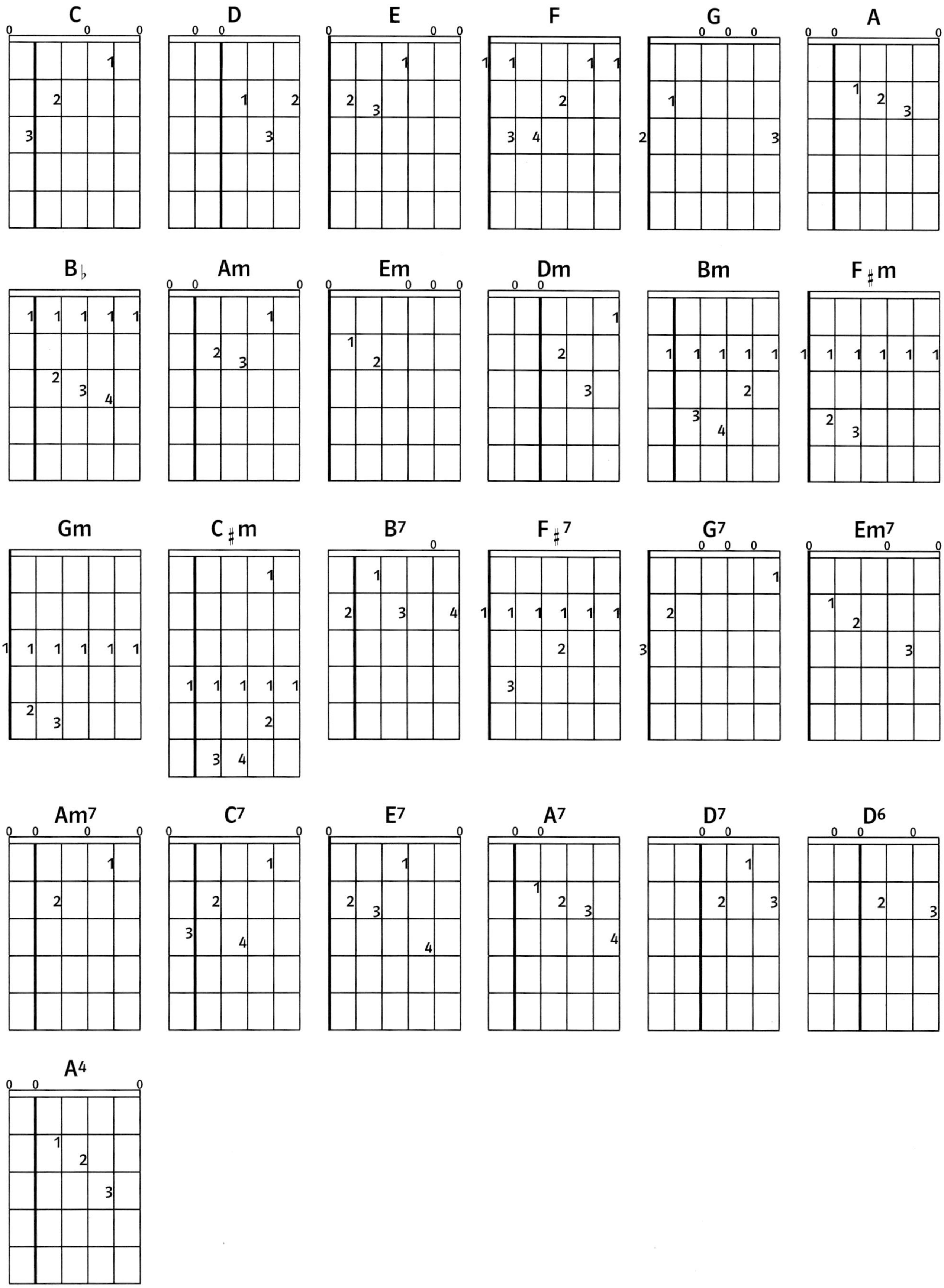

Tracklist

Track	Title	Copy master	Duration
1	Inky Minky Tinky	1	2:53
2	World Harvest	2	2:43
3	Mr Weatherman	6	3:16
4	Witch Watch	10	2:11
5	The Ghosts of the Sea	13	2:38
6	I like the fireworks	15	1:58
7	We wish you a merry Christmas	17	1:46
8	Mary's boy-child	23	2:34
9	Auld Lang Syne	24	1:56
10	In Winter	29	2:32
11	Valentine Songs	25	3:06
12	Shrove Tuesday	36	1:20
13	Carnival Nights	39	3:21
14	Spring is coming	41	1:54
15	April Fool	45	2:08
16	The Easter Bunnies	46	0:48
17	May Morning	50	1:17
18	Happy Birthday	54	2:23
19	Muscles	57	4:02
20	To-do at the Zoo	60	3:06
21	Holiday	64	1:51

Composers:

Peter Ehlebracht; Jean Gilbert; Bernhard Hering/Wolfgang Hering/Bernd Meyerholz; Jane Morgan; Robert Metcalf; Bernhard Hering; traditional

Musicians

Bernhard Hering:	drums, keyboards, vibraphone, bass, percussion
Martin Wester:	guitar, keyboards, bass, percussion
Robert Metalf:	vocals, guitar (In Winter, Happy Birthday)
Brigitte Schanz-Hering:	vocals
Thomas Dolle:	clarinet (The Weatherman)
Harald Wehnhardt:	guitar (The Weatherman)

Arrangements

Wolfgang E. Hering/Bernhard Hering/Martin Wester
Harald Wehnhardt

Produced and arranged by Klangraum & Wolgang Hering.
Recorded at Klangraum Studio, Mainz (Germany).